Beyond Ballyhoo

Beyond Ballyhoo

Motion Picture
Promotion and Gimmicks

by
MARK THOMAS McGEE

McFarland & Company, Inc., Publishers
Jefferson, North Carolina, and London

British Library Cataloguing-in-Publication data available

Library of Congress Cataloguing-in-Publication Data

McGee, Mark Thomas, 1947–
 Beyond ballyhoo.

 Bibliography: p. 225.
 Filmography: p. 195.
 Includes index.
 1. Advertising—Motion pictures. 2. Cinema-
tography—Special effects. I. Title.
HF6161.M7M36 1989   659.1'979143   89-42731

ISBN 0-89950-435-3 (lib. bdg. : 50# alk. paper) ∞

Printed in the United States of America

McFarland & Company, Inc., Publishers
 Box 611, Jefferson, North Carolina 28640

*For Dave Allen, who didn't get
a "Hypnotic Eye" balloon either*

Table of Contents

Preface

At last, the shocking truth can finally be told! This is the book that takes you beyond anything your mind has ever imagined, beyond the reaches of time and space itself, *Beyond Ballyhoo*. This is the one you've been hearing about, the book that Hollywood tried to stop! Because this is the book that rips the lid off of the twisted world of advertising where deception knows no limit and disappointment no end. As one victim after another is sucked into a miasma of gimmicks and giveaways you won't believe your eyes!

You'll SHUDDER when you read about one studio's scheme to hoodwink exhibitors across the nation! You'll GASP at the nerve of the director who faked a Nazi attack on his theatre to save his failing play! You'll SHIVER at the insidious thing called PsychoRama! Absolutely no punches pulled! *Beyond Ballyhoo* will hit you like no other book you've ever read! It'll grab your guts and pull them right through your mouth!

What is the secret of the Erotiphile card? Can its fuzzy coating actually cause someone to become obsessed with horrible desires like *The*

Horrible Dr. Hitchcock? What were the contents of the *Slitthis* Survival Kit? How many women actually wore the bellybutton jewels they were given when they saw *Judy's Little No-No*? Were any of the selections on the *Children Shouldn't Play with Dead Things* Gourmet Ghoul Menu? When the Devil are they going to announce the million dollar winner of the *Million Dollar Mystery*? These and other urgent questions are completely overlooked in *Beyond Ballyhoo*, a story so big it took these people to tell it:

    Marty Kearns . . . It was only a matter of time until the conventions got the better of him!

    Bob Villard . . . He'd sell his soul for a *She-Creature* pressbook!

    R.J. Robertson . . . Living with the fear that people might mistake him for a relative of Pat Robertson!

    Don Glut . . . Brave enough to tell the shameful memory that's haunted him so long!

    Wendy Wright . . . Can she resist *The Hypnotic Eye*?

    Fred Olen Ray . . . Filmmaker by day, lover of sleazy cinema by night!

Warning! This book, except for the pages of this Preface, is treated with Complete-O, an amazing new ink that compels the reader to finish the text in one sitting! So if you think your nerves can take it, read *Beyond Ballyhoo*. And if you find that Complete-O doesn't work . . . Oh well.

Mark McGee,
Duarte, California
April, 1989

Its trade, which is in dreams at so many dollars a thousand feet, is managed by business men pretending to be artists and by artists pretending to be business men. In this queer atmosphere, nobody stays as he was; the artist begins to lose his art, and the business man becomes temperamental and unbalanced.

—J.B. Priestley

One

She Was a Plant, of Course

Walking along the midway, with a corn dog in one hand and a Coke in the other, you pass a row of tents and booths peopled with shrill-voiced hucksters, each with only one thought — to separate you from your money. Promises of amazing, incredible, fantastic, mind-boggling, one-of-a-kind whatchamacallits fill the air as these shameless con artists cajole and bully you. But you're too smart for them. Without breaking your stride you casually take another bite of your corn dog and pass right by "the world's only living unicorn" because they can't fool you. You know it's just a goat with a horn glued to its head. And who in their right mind would want to see the "world's fattest man" anyway? No, Sir. Two bits is two bits. No sense throwing it away.

On you go, feeling a little proud of yourself. There's a smile on your face that wasn't there before. You're in control and it feels good. But then you pass a guy who swears he's got a live, two-headed creature from outer space. You wonder, as your determination to ignore him weakens, what exactly the liar has behind the tent. Not that you believe

1

he has what he says he has. That would be a subversion of your principles of understanding. A creature from space would be under scientific observation. It would have been on the news and on the cover of every magazine. You KNOW it's a con. It can't be anything else. But what? That's all you want to know. And the only way to find out . . .

Showmanship. That's what this book is all about. All of the stuff that movie producers and publicity departments dreamed up to separate the sucker from his money.

My father told me a joke about a guy who was casually strolling across a field one lazy afternoon when he happened upon a farmer who was beating a mule across its head with a baseball bat. The man was appalled and bridged quickly the distance between himself and the farmer to ask what the devil the farmer thought he was doing. The farmer took another whack at the mule's head and politely turned to the man and said, "I've got to get ol' Hector here back into the barn." The farmer's manner was calm which only confused the stranger even more. He told the farmer that he didn't understand how beating the poor animal was going to get it back in the barn, to which the farmer replied matter-of-factly, "Well, I have to get his attention first." Which is precisely the way the ballyhoo artist begins his (or her) efforts to extract money, by getting the attention of the intended victim. The flamboyant Howard Hughes knew how to do it well enough. He may not have been able to make a good movie but he sure knew how to sell a bad one. His stunt for Underwater (1955) was nothing short of brilliant. He held the premiere of the film at Silver Springs, Florida . . . under water! The audience wore aqua lungs and diving masks. The event was covered by 211 reporters and columnists from Hollywood to New York. Exhibitors were drooling. Within 24 hours after the story broke they were on the phone to RKO to book the picture.

When the original Frankenstein premiered in Chicago in 1931, the manager of the State Lake Theatre dressed an actor in a monster costume and sent him parading about the town with the actor's wife several feet behind him clutching a device that supposedly controlled her husband's actions. The couple happened upon a woman who took the whole thing seriously and fainted. They got her attention all right.

The earliest motion pictures didn't need gimmicks like monsters and underwater premieres to attract people's attention. During those formative years when motion pictures were penny arcade peep shows

What may look like some sort of torture device is actually the first film studio. This photograph was taken in 1893.

they *were* the gimmick. And when they grew in length and began to tell stories they were used as gimmicks to attract people to vaudeville shows. Years later, vaudeville shows were used to support the movies.

Initially, Thomas Edison invented the motion picture to supplement the phonograph. Author Paul Rotha notes: "It is extraordinary to observe that this ambition of Edison, which brought the film into being, is precisely the opposite to the aim of the present-day producer, who attempts to supplement his visual images with their recorded sounds. This astonishing fact is worth serious consideration. The visual film was thought necessary to accompany the sound record. Fifty years later, sound is deemed necessary to accompany the visual film. Many dialog films made since 1930 have been, in fact, glorified, illustrated, gramophone records." (*The Film Till Now*, Hamlyn Pub., rev. ed. 1967, pp. 67–68.)

Edison's moving pictures could only be seen by one person at a time, through the peephole of his Kinetoscope machine. And in those days "moving pictures" was all they were, scenes of dancers or boxers or anything that moved, generally no longer than fifty feet in length. But that was enough. Then Thomas Armat invented a machine that could project the film image on a large screen. Armat called his machine the

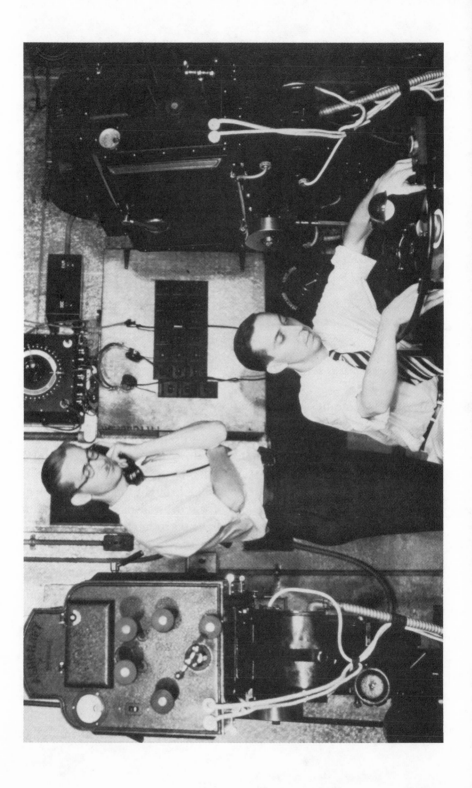

When Al Jolson dropped to his knees to sing "Mammy," he warbled the silent film swan song (The Jazz Singer, Warner Bros., 1927).

Vitascope. Edison didn't like it and not for the reason the you might think. It wasn't jealousy. Edison thought mass showings would satiate people's appetites for motion pictures.

An early advertisement for Vitascope was much more accurate in its prediction for the future of the media. The ad said that Armat's machine would cause an impact "more far-reaching, scientific and advantageous" than Edison or anyone else could possibly imagine and promised mega-profits to those people who had the sense to control it. Vitascope was given its first demonstration in Georgia at the 1895 Cotton States' Exposition. Thirty years later 100 million people spent $750 million at the 20,000 theaters across the country. By then moving pictures were no longer a gimmick, but each embellishment upon them was. Two items that audiences take for granted these days—sound and color—were once considered gimmicks. Heavily criticized gimmicks.

(Opposite) *Using the Vitaphone system (sound on discs), two Paramount technicians play back a test.*

Try to imagine what it must have been like to hear movies talking for the first time and you'll realize that sound, more than color, was the greatest movie gimmick of them all. So great, in fact, that it transformed from a novelty to a necessity at a swifter rate than the motion picture itself. Warner Brothers premiered *The Jazz Singer* in 1927. By 1930 it would have been ridiculous to read an ad like the one for Fox's *The Ghost Talks*, released the year before, which proudly noted that "Everybody Talks!" By 1930 audiences expected nothing less. A guy like Charlie Chaplin may have been able to get away with making silent movies but there were few others who could.

In an age of stereophonic Dolby sound it may be impossible to truly understand the stringent opposition that accompanied the arrival of sound. There were a lot of reasons stated but at the bottom of them all was the fear that sound would ruin the magic of motion pictures by making them too realistic, a groundless fear as anyone who has ever seen a Chuck Norris movie can testify to, but it was something that people believed.

Experiments with talking pictures began in 1890. Some of Edison's Kinetoscopes had sound. But it was sound from a disc and it was impossible to keep it in synch with the film. The problem was how to put the sound on the film and it took many people* working separately and collectively to find the solution. Typically, once the solution was found there was no one around to applaud their efforts. Movie moguls weren't interested in sound movies just as they weren't initially interested in wide screen movies or 3-D movies, which you'll read about in chapters Three and Four. William Fox, the president of Fox Pictures, went so far as to throw out the sound equipment installed in six of his theaters. Make no mistake about it, sound movies were born out of desperation, not from any farsighted Hollywood visionary as an old *Screenland* article claimed. Also typically, once the gamble paid off, and in spite of the popular sentiment among these Hollywood visionaries that sound

---

A few of the people responsible for the development of sound on film are: A.G. Bell, C.A. Bell, and S. Tainer who recorded light from sound through a fine slit in 1886; C.J. Hohenstein who used a method similar to General Electric's to put sound on film in 1887; J. Poliakoff who used positive film images with a photoelectric cell in 1900; Ernst Ruhmer with his Photographophon in 1901; Eugene Lauste who was unable to develop his sound on film system because of the outbreak of World War I; Lee De Forest who invented the audion amplifier in 1906; Theodore Case and Earl Sponable who developed the sound camera in 1923.

movies were nothing but a passing fad (or gimmick if you will), every studio in town inserted talking sequences into their already completed silent productions.

One of the interesting paradoxes of the motion picture business is that everyone in it wants to be the first with something new except they want someone else to try it first. Fox may have lagged behind Warner

Brothers a bit but the company did make the first all-talking feature shot outdoors and the first all-talking farce-comedy. In a silly attempt to butt in front of the line, Paramount embarrassed itself by claiming its *Interference* (1928) was the first *quality* all-talking feature. One of the principal players in that film, Clive Brook, described his disconcerting experience of working on a sound movie for the first time to *The New York Times*: "I found that the microphone is more difficult to face than the most hardened audience; I was conscious of a metallic little instrument hanging like a sword of Damocles over my head . . . my voice sounded unfamiliar to my ears, every word was oddly muffled; there was no echo, no resonance. Two ominous, tank-like objects were focused on me. Faces peered at me from the darkness inside these caverns. I caught the reflection of camera lenses in the plate-glass windows that form the front walls of these 'tanks.' Cameras were grinding, but the sound of their mechanism had been silenced. Not even the familiar splutter of the klieg lights could be heard for they had been supplanted by huge banks of incandescent lamps. The director cannot even tell us when to start; we must watch a monitor man who waves his hand for us to begin.

"I find myself starting off in the declamatory fashion of the stage. I was not thinking in terms of microphone sensitivity or the tremendous amplification of the apparatus. When I had finished, technicians turned on the record they had just made; I heard a deep, strange voice come booming out of the loudspeakers. It was not, I told myself, Clive Brook. It alternately faded into nothingness and then rang out in a thunderous crescendo. [Roy] Pomeroy [head of Paramount's sound department] smiled at me. 'Was that my voice?' I asked. 'Yes, but you couldn't recognize it, could you? Try it again,' he said, 'and this time speak just as you would in a small room at home. Don't think of playing to the gallery; you don't have to project; the gallery doesn't exist here.' After I did it the next time, I heard the voice in the loudspeakers again. This time it was unmistakably my own. Although it was not loud, somehow it seemed to fill every corner of the huge room. I had learned my first lesson in microphone recording."

Critic Kenneth Macgowan wrote, "It was doubly fortunate for the Hollywood studios that they had all taken to sound before the depression that began in the fall of 1929. The Wall Street boom and the quick success of the talkies enabled exhibitors to borrow and then pay back the money needed for new sound equipment; the cost ran from $8,500 to $20,000. If the producers had waited till late October, 1929 — as they

HEAR HER RUN the SCALE of HUMAN EMOTION *via* VITAPHONE

Irresistible.... FANNIE BRICE _in_ "*My Man*"

See and Hear this charming Comedienne in her varying moods

Hear Fannie Brice sing "*My Man*"—"*I'd rather be Blue over You*"—"*I'm an Indian*"—"*Second-hand Rose*" —"*If you want the Rainbow, You must have the Rain*"—songs that run the entire scale of human emotion—that strike responsive chords in every heart.

"*My Man*" is a tense drama, full of tragedy and comedy. It will bring tears—laughter —love—to every audience.

Again Vitaphone makes history—brings to you America's premiere comedienne—*Fannie Brice in* "*My Man*."

See and hear this famous star sing the songs that have thrilled audiences the world over. You will be captivated with her inimitable humor. Moved by her tender pathos. Lifted to soul-stirring emotional climaxes, as she triumphs over lost love and gains the love of millions.

The world today acknowledges the leadership of Warner Brothers Vitaphone Talking Pictures. Vitaphone success has swept this country. It has aroused unprecedented demonstrations of approval in the capitals of Europe. It has enkindled a degree of public enthusiasm never even approached in any other form of entertainment. *Decide now* you will see and hear *Fannie Brice in "My Man."*

The Characters act and *Talk* like *living people*

"*My Man*" is a 100% Vitaphone Talking Picture — every character in the play *alive* with voice and action! Remember—that Vitaphone is an exclusive product of Warner Bros.—that you can see and hear Vitaphone *only* in Warner Bros. and First National Pictures.

Make no mistake. Be sure it's either a Warner Bros. or a First National Picture — then you'll KNOW it's VITAPHONE.

⟦ IF THERE IS NOT A THEATRE IN YOUR COMMUNITY EQUIPPED AS YET TO SHOW "MY MAN" AS A TALKING PICTURE—BE SURE TO SEE IT AS A SILENT PICTURE ⟧

might well have done except for the daring of Warner Brothers and Fox—sound would have been impossible for ten more years ..." (*Behind the Screen: The History and Techniques of the Motion Picture*, Delacorte 1969, p. 287).

No doubt the actors and actresses whose voices didn't match their appearance wished it had. Volumes have been written about the famous silent screen stars displaced by sound, an unfortunate condition that Hollywood could laugh about twenty years later in *Singin' in the Rain* (1952) but at the time it was serious business. For those who knew they couldn't cut it, the success of *The Jazz Singer* must have been as welcome as the San Francisco earthquake, even though the prevailing attitude was that sound was a gimmick the public would soon grow weary of. Even the critics who wrote favorable reviews of the movie treated the sound aspect of it like a seasoning—too much or too little could be dangerous. To show you what I mean here are excerpts from two reviews of the period, the first written by Louella Parsons and the second by some anonymous writer at *The New York Times*:

"The strong protests uttered against the Vitaphone as a destroyer of the peaceful silence of the motion picture, suffered a glorious defeat last night. Without the Vitaphone 'The Jazz Singer' would not have so completely won over the large audience at the Criterion Theater.

"'The Jazz Singer' and the Vitaphone are affinities that do not jangle out of tune. If there had been long conversations and more attempts at vocal comedy, the effect would not have been so satisfactory. But very wisely Warner Brothers, save for a single scene between Al Jolsen and his mother, eliminated the spoken word. But the singing! Think of hearing Al Jolsen sing the words of his songs as a part of the screen play.

"The combination exceeded this reviewer's best expectations. I have been one who has lamented the encroachment of the voice in the silent drama.

"'The Jazz Singer,' therefore, comes as an agreeable surprise. I must right here make it clear that there are few pictures that lend themselves so perfectly to the synchronization of music as 'The Jazz Singer'"(*New York Times*, April, 1929).

The *Times*: "The Vitaphoned songs and some dialogue have been introduced most adroitly. This in itself is an ambitious move, for in the expression of song the Vitaphone vitalizes the production enormously. The dialogue is not so effective, for it does not always catch the nuances of speech or inflections of the voice so that one is not aware of the mechanical features.

"The Warner Brothers astutely realized that a film conception of 'The Jazz Singer' was one of the few subjects that would lend itself to the use of the Vitaphone . . ."(*New York Times*, April, 1929).

The idea that only certain subjects "lend" themselves to sound is sort of like the actress who states emphatically that she'll only do a scene in the buff if it's integral to the story. Personally, I think a good set of hooters is integral to just about any story but what's the difference? It isn't a question of whether it's integral or not. If a producer thinks the audience will pay to see a set of hooters then hooters is what they'll get. You can bet the Warner Brothers weren't losing sleep over picking a property that would "lend itself to the use of the Vitaphone." They were trying to save their studio.

Sound didn't come about as a natural growth of film art but because Warner Brothers needed a gimmick to save them from bankruptcy. As it turned out they couldn't have done better for themselves. *The Jazz Singer* outgrossed all of the competition, despite the fact that there were only a few theaters equipped to run sound movies.

"At last, pictures that talk like living people!" exclaimed an ad:

> Vitaphone Talking Pictures
> are electrifying audiences the country over!

For Vitaphone brings to you the greatest of the world's great entertainers . . . Screen stars! Stage stars! Opera stars! Famous or- chestras! Master musicians!

> Vitaphone recreates them ALL before your eyes.
> You see and hear them act, talk, sing and play—
> like human beings in the flesh!

Do not confuse Vitaphone with mere "sound effects."

Vitaphone is the ONE proved successful talking picture—exclusive product of Warner Bros.

Remember this—if it's not Warner Bros. Vitaphone, it's NOT the real, life-like talking picture.

Vitaphone climaxes all previous entertainment achievements.

See and hear this marvel of the age—Vitaphone.

In 1952 director Russell Rouse made a film titled *The Thief.* It con- tained no dialog, which was so unusual that it was considered a gimmick film. Mel Brooks attempted a similar experiment with *Silent Movie* (1976). Neither film was particularly successful, either artistically or financially, but in both cases the absence of sound was a gimmick, the reverse of the way it all began. Similarly, in the early days color was con- sidered a gimmick. These days black and white is a gimmick.

There's a big hoopla being made today about colorized movies, whereby color is added to black and white films via computer, giving these old classics the look of hand-tinted post cards. Ted Turner, who gutted M-G-M to get at its film library, is largely responsible for this new

What can YOU find in "SULLIVAN'S TRAVELS"?
Solve this - and WIN PRIZES!

Take a trip through this word maze—and find for yourself what Sullivan (Joel McCrea) discovered on his travels! Win a prize with a correct answer! If you do it correctly, you'll learn exactly what it is that Joel McCrea, as the

movie producer "Sullivan" in Preston Sturges' new comedy-drama success, "Sullivan's Travels," found out after a series of delightful adventures around the country with gorgeous Veronica Lake.

It's simple. Work the maze the same as you would a crossword puzzle. If you do it correctly, you will develop a series of words in the "road" in the diagram which, when placed together, give you, in sentence form, the message which McCrea

discovered. It's the message that he puts to good use in the picture, as you'll learn when you see this delightful comedy when it comes to the.......... Theatre on............next!

Get going now! Guest ticket awards—a pair to each of the first (——) persons who turn in the correct answers—will be awarded at the......... Theatre on......next! Here are the definitions:

DEFINITIONS

Horizontal

1. Word of interrogation
4. Water conveyances
9. North Moroccan tribesman
13. To turn rapidly
16. Front upper part of head
17. Subject of sermon
18. Pointed end
21. Girl's name
23. King of beasts
26. Dove's home
27. Personal pronoun
28. A weed
29. Bounding lines
31. To blend by heat
33. Sitting in a nest
36. Spoken
37. Seaman's tale
38. Hat making material
39. Part of verb "to be"
41. Eskimos' homes
42. Big city in Brazil
44. Wants
45. Old

48. Horse-drawn vehicle
50. Manuscript (Abbr.)
51. Member of Parliament (Abbr.)
52. Popular planet
53. Alive
54. Not bad
55. Snarl
56. Female sheep
57. A passing by
58. Audible manifestation of glee

Vertical

1. Deceives
2. Public dwelling
3. Inspiring awe
4. Form of verb "to be"
5. Draught animal
6. Near
7. Heavenly body
8. Scotch head covering
9. —avis—
10. Scotch dance
11. Fish's propellor

12. Article
14. Baked dainty
15. Negative
16. Before Christ
17. Demonstrative pronoun
19. Persia
20. Famous volcano
22. Periods of time
24. Bone
25. Electric lighting device
28. Implements
30. Verdure
31. Faith (Spanish)
32. Nazi bomber
34. Spinning toy
35. Become larger
39. Eagerly curious
40. Folk tale
41. Minor devil
43. Anger
46. Hen's product
47. Female deer
49. African antelope
52. Us
53. Part of verb "to be"

Like the lottery, a theater ticket was often an opportunity to get rich quick. (Paramount, 1941.)

movement, and claims that it's breathing life into the old movies. It may well be but there are those who feel this sort of tampering is as vile and unforgivable as painting a mustache on the Mona Lisa. Fortunately, for those who are offended, this "breakthrough" is accomplished on video tape and can only be seen on a monitor, giving the viewer the option of simply tuning the sickly looking color out.

This colorization business is nothing new. Directors were doing it as far back as 1894, only then it was done by hand. Film pioneer D.W. Griffith tinted certain portions of *Way Down East* (1920) and George Méliès did the same to many of his films. As you might expect, hand-tinting was rather time-consuming so alternate, less painstaking methods of adding color were quickly explored. A fellow in England by the name of George Albert Smith patented his Kinemacolor process in 1909. Smith believed he could achieve a color of sorts by projecting a black and white film at twice the normal speed through a wheel with a red-orange and blue-green filter that spun like a propeller. After sitting through Smith's 2½-hour documentary the only effects truly achieved were eyestrain and nausea.

A couple of guys in America had a better idea. Daniel Comstock and Herbert Kalmus used filters too, only they put them in a camera with two apertures. Their efforts weren't immediately successful but they kept at it and in 1922 *Toll of the Sea* was released in something the two men called Technicolor. It employed two film strips, one dyed blue-green, the other red-orange, which were utlimately married on a single film strip. The color wasn't quite right but it was good enough to make it fashionable for filmmakers to include color sequences in their otherwise black and white productions.

Some people were thrilled by the sudden burst of color during *The Ten Commandments* (1923).* Others were dismayed. Some people felt color confused the audience, that it distracted the viewer from the story. But Comstock and Kalmus weren't distracted or confused. They continued to improve their color technique, finally adding a third color, made possible by the development of the beam-splitter camera. The beam-splitter divided the colors of a single image onto three separate negatives—one for green, blue and red. This not only made the colors richer but enabled the folks at the lab to play with the intensity of each color the way a painter mixes paints. This control made Technicolor the most sought after color process in Hollywood for years. It was first used on a short subject that has since fallen into the public domain called *La Cucaracha* (1933). *Becky Sharp* was the first feature to use it.

For the poverty row filmmaker, however, the price of Technicolor was prohibitive. English-born William Thomas provided a viable alter-

---

Color sequences were also in The Phantom of the Opera *(1925),* Ben Hur *(1926),* The Wedding March *(1928),* The Desert Song *(1929), and* Chasing Rainbows *(1930).*

native with his Cinecolor, which cost about 25 percent more than regular black and white film. But it was a two-color system so the color wasn't true and the image was a little fuzzy but you get what you pay for.

For years, even after the less expensive Eastman three-color process was introduced in the early 1950s, color was often treated as a novelty or gimmick. It wasn't taken for granted so quickly the way sound was. And one of the finest examples of "gimmick color" was *The Wizard of Oz* (1939) which used color to contrast the magical land of Oz with the sepiatone drabness of Kansas. M-G-M repeated this magical concept of color to enhance *The Secret Garden* (1949). Several films in the '40s contained color sequences. *Irene* (1940) had one of its musical sequences in color as were the battle scenes at the end of *Task Force* (1949). Other movies were stingier. Only the last scene in *Portrait of Jenny* (1948) was in color, a shot of the portrait itself as was the last moment of *The Solid Gold Cadillac* (1956). There were also snippets of color in the 1945 *The Picture of Dorian Gray*.

During the days of silent films it wasn't unusual to see night sequences tinted blue. Although tinting seemed passé after the arrival of Technicolor, there were a few soundies that included tinted sequences. During a storm sequence in the already mentioned *Portrait of Jenny* the color green was employed for mood, as it was during the Leprechaun forest sequences in *The Luck of the Irish* (1948) and when Cesar Romero discovered *The Lost Continent* (1951) with its Gumby-like prehistoric monsters.

Red highlighted the battle scenes in *Hell's Angels* (1930), the orphanage fire at the conclusion of *Mighty Joe Young* (1949), the Martian landscape in *Rocketship X-M* (1950), and the burst of gunfire from the business end of the weapon held by Leo G. Carroll at the climax of Alfred Hitchcock's *Spellbound* (1945). Both *A Midsummer Night's Dream* (1935) and *A Day at the Races* (1937) contained blue-tinted sequences and a number of movies — *The Ghost Goes West* (1936), *The Firefly, Maytime* (both 1937), *The Rains Came, The Girl of the Golden West, Bad Man of Brimstone* (all 1938), *The Oklahoma Kid, Of Mice and Men* (both 1939) and some of the Jungle Jim movies made by Columbia* — were in sepia.

Perhaps all of the Jungle Jim movies were in sepia but I can only attest to the one I saw, Jungle Moon Men (1955), believing it was a science fiction film. Let us not dwell on my disappointment.

When the price of color was prohibitive, some producers tinted sequences in their movies. (Top) Osa Massen, John Emery, Hugh O'Brien, and Lloyd Bridges see red on the planet Mars in Rocketship X-M (Lippert, 1950). (Bottom) Acquanetta is shocked to find everything on The Lost Continent has turned green (Lippert, 1951).

Producers of inexpensive science fiction films during the 1950s discovered they could splice a minute or less of color footage to the climax of their black and white productions and advertise them in such a way as to give the impression the entire thing was in color. Guilty as charged is producer Herman Cohen with his *I Was a Teenage Franken-stein* (1957), Bert I. Gordon with *War of the Colossal Beast* and Al (*Robot Monster*) Zimbalist with his stock footage extravaganza *The Monster from Green Hell* (both 1958). To compound the insult the color on these films tended to be on the red side, the first two because they were pro-cessed by the Pathé lab, which seemed to favor red, and the third because of an accident during the filming of the climax.

Like many sci fi films of the '50s, *The Monster from Green Hell* was about atomic mutations, in this particular case gigantic wasps loose in Africa. The reason producer Zimbalist chose this local was because he'd purchased a lot of stock footage from *Stanley and Livingston* (1939). He also had some stock footage of erupting volcanoes — ergo the wasps are covered in lava at the end of the story. To this end a large miniature cavern set was constructed, populated with lots of wasp puppets. With two cameras to capture the action, a bunch of oatmeal (dyed red) was poured on the set. In the middle of it all special effects ace Irving Block became frantic, afraid that things didn't look hot enough. He began throwing chunks of dry ice at the set, so much so that he completely obliterated the image on one camera and the other captured, in slow motion, his hands flinging the dry ice. The set and the wasps were destroyed and with no money left to build them again the only thing left to do was reprint the black and white shots of the wasps already filmed, dye them red and matte lava into the bottom of the frame. It looked lousy but fans of '50s sci fi films were used to that.

How to Make a Monster (1958), again from producer Cohen, gave the audience a little more color for its money, the entire last reel, about twelve minutes' worth, though it is doubtful that 3-D and Dolby sound could have gotten the thing up on its feet.

As color gradually phased out black and white, desperate ballyhooers attempted to keep its novelty factor alive by inventing new names like Exoticolor and LunaColor but eventually color was taken for granted just like sound and there wasn't anything the con artists could do about it. They had to come up with new gimmicks. Fortunately they did or I'd be in big trouble for the remainder of this book. And now that I've got color and sound out of the way we can get on with the good stuff.

Let's jump ahead to 1966 and a little something called *The Monsters Invade the Pajama Party*. It will come as no surprise to you, I'm sure, to learn that this was a truly terrible movie. It wasn't even a feature really. I think it ran about 40 or 45 minutes, which was plenty long enough. I went to this thing, old enough to know better, and got exactly what I deserved. The advertisements for this movie swore that without the aid of 3-D glasses the monsters would come off the screen . . . and into the audience. I knew it would be a gyp but it was that damn two-headed creature from outer space. I had to see for myself.

If there was a plot I have forgotten it. The only thing I can recall is there were a bunch of young people, non-actors of course, talking each other to death in what must have been an old deserted house. They were probably there on a dare or a scavenger hunt, but whatever the excuse there was a mad doctor in this house who was conducting some kind of wicked experiment, and toward the climax he sent his henchmen into the audience to gather up a fresh guinea pig. The henchmen walked off camera and came from behind the screen, into the audience, grabbed a woman in the front row, carried her behind the screen and reappeared with her on camera. She was a plant, of course. A shill. But it shook everyone up for a moment. They got a buck and a quarter out of me. But I was too smart for 'em to expect to get my money's worth.

I later learned that this was not even an original gag. It had been done before at some theater in San Francisco in the early '50s. It may have been done before that. The point is it was another gimmick and some people that afternoon may have felt they got their money's worth. It was different. Surprising. A piece of showmanship.

Two

Can You Take Percepto?

*When considering the commercialism which surrounds
the producing and exhibiting of any one film, the un-
scrupulous dealings and double-crossing which occur
when a production is launched, it is surprising to discover how far the cinema has really advanced as a
medium of dramatic expression.*
—Paul Rotha

The marquee of the downtown Los Angeles theater read *Poor
White Trash* (1961) and the line to see it wrapped around the corner. It
was like the old days when the theater ran top attractions at the top
prices. The city had gone gray, since, and ugly iron bars had grown on
all the storefronts. An apt setting for a movie that promised to be
naughty. Actually, it *promised* nothing but suggested plenty. Nary a clue
was given as to what the picture was about. Except they couldn't show
scenes from it on television and armed guards were keeping the
children out. It just *had* to be naughty. Except that it wasn't.

"I don't sell a piece of goods, I sell a concept," Humphrey Bogart told Leo G. Carroll in *We're No Angels* (1955), a sentiment that should hang on the wall of any publicity department you pick. It relieves the painful burden of particulars that so often bind creativity. In advertising the actual product is sometimes barely mentioned, which leads to some confusion. The kind of confusion that a movie promoter can turn to advantage.

In 1956 M.A. Ripps made a picture called *Bayou* (1956), which was released by United Artists who used it as a supporting feature. It did little business. When U.A.'s contract ran out and the film became Ripps' property he added new scenes to the picture and sent it back out as *Poor White Trash* with an ambiguous advertising campaign that could only lead to shattered expectations. The only truly provocative scene came from the original version, a rather peculiar dance performed by Timothy Carey. It's not so much a case of let the buyer beware as it is let 'em be damned. It worked so well that Ripps was back with it ten years later, on the same bill with its sequel, which really wasn't a sequel at all. Ripps had a new pitch. For unstated reasons Ripps objected to the films' being shown together. Supposedly the matter was in court. The public was urged to act quickly before the court took action. And Ripps made money again. And *still* the most provocative thing about the program was Tim Carey's dance.

A showman who would have applauded Ripps' boldness was Kroger Babb who may have been the one to invent the "armed guard" stunt when he released *Mom and Dad* back in 1945.

"The film was not all that sensational," said Joe Solomon, once Babb's booking agent in the Philadelphia area. "We had nurses in the lobby. They weren't really nurses but nobody knew the difference. We separated the crowds which added to the mystique. Women in the afternoon and the guys in the evening. That was an old gag too but it always worked." Solomon beefed up attendance in his area by making sure there was a photographer on hand to catch the pale-faced audience staggering from an afternoon showing, suffering the effects of something that Solomon had tossed into the ventilation system. The resulting article mentioned nothing about the fetid air and left the cause to the imagination of the readers who rushed to the theater to take the dare. No movie's gonna make me sick. The same gag was used to sell *The Exorcist* (1973) except people actually *were* getting sick.

The most sensational thing about *Mom and Dad* was the footage of a baby's birth that Kroger Babb added to it. The movie was about a teenage romance that led to an unwanted pregnancy and a plea by a sympathetic teacher for sex education in the schools. It was directed by veteran William Beaudine who (rumor has it) often fell asleep during scenes (for which one could hardly blame him). Babb's baby footage got the film banned in Chicago which couldn't have delighted Babb more. Audiences were warned to see it quick before it was banned in their state. Sound familiar?

Kroger Babb was an old-time barnstormer, born in Lees Creek, Ohio, who called himself "The Fearless Showman." He formed Hallmark Productions 1945 which catered to audiences seeking the sensational. *The Devil's Weed* (1949, also known as *Wild Weed*) was a Hallmark film, billed as an exposé of the "marijuana" racket. Lila Leeds, an aspiring actress who'd been busted for smoking pot with Robert Mitchum, was the star. It's the sort of casting that low budget films do best, yet another hint of sleaze, the film equivalent of a gossip magazine, never as scandalous as it pretends to be. It lends some credibility to the theory that most films are made for advertisements, not audiences.

"Perhaps Hallmark has never had a fine motion picture," Babb remarked, "yet it has never distributed an attraction that wasn't thoroughly exploited, bringing exhibitors millions of extra dollars."

Sam Goldwyn and David Selznick were considered showmen of the highest calibre. A body could be sure of a lavish production if nothing else. William Castle is at the other end of the stick but no less a showman. Goldwyn and Selznick put everything they had on the screen. Castle took it off the screen and put it into the audience, in a tireless effort to make the audience a part of the action on the screen.

Born William Schloss in 1914, Castle got into show business running errands for a Broadway producer. As he tells it, he learned the value of a good gimmick on a play he directed called *Not for Children*. Tickets were backing up and it looked like the show was dead before it opened when the playhouse was attacked by vandals who broke windows and painted swastikas on the walls. A newspaper article explained that the play's leading lady, Ellen Schwanneke, had declined Hitler's request to return to Germany. Tickets sold out after that. Even an ill wind blows someone good fortune. Right? Would you be shocked to learn that it was more than chance? Castle was the one who marked the walls and broke the windows. The idea occurred to him after his leading lady

Lovely Lita Milan's acting career practically began and ended with her perfor-
mance in Bayou, *retitled* Poor White Trash. *(Photograph by Bert Six, Warner*
Bros., 1958.)

was asked to be Hitler's guest at an arts festival. She wasn't interested
and Castle offered to send her regrets to Adolf. He sent a cablegram,
on Ms. Schwanneke's behalf, telling Hitler that she wanted no part of
him or his government, a copy of which Castle hand-carried to the New
York papers. Along with the pictures of the damaged playhouse.

Castle directed bread and butter programmers for Columbia and
Universal for years before he struck out on his own to become a producer. He hooked up with writer Robb White while they were working
together on the *Men of Annapolis* television series. Having recently seen
a French suspense film called *Diabolique* (1955), Castle thought he'd try

The fearless showman himself, Kroger Babb.

his hand at a suspense picture and with money from White and from hocking his home, Castle and White made *Macabre* (1958), based on a book called *The Marble Orchard*, written as a gag by twelve authors.

Macabre suffered a serious problem for a suspense picture. It had no suspense. White knew it. Castle knew it. And so did the people at Allied Artists when they agreed to buy the picture from Castle at more than twice what he'd spent plus a percentage. They weren't buying Castle's movie. They were buying his gimmick. Castle got Lloyds of London to insure each member of the audience for $1000 if they suffered death by fright.

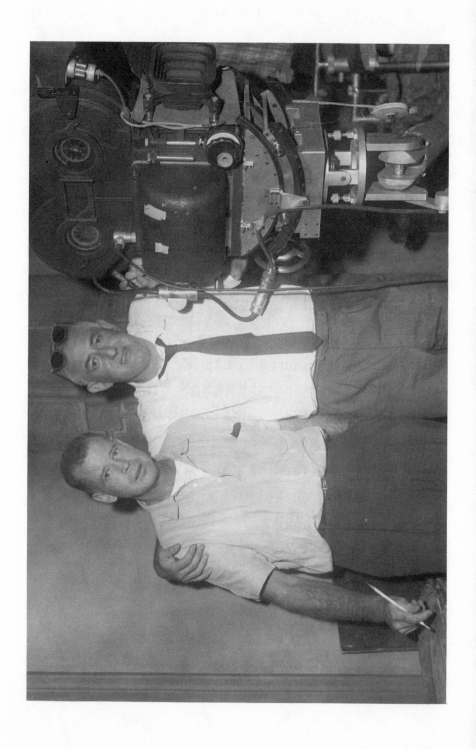

And this is "Emergo," the amazing new wonder where the "thrills fly right into the audience!" Taken during a screening of House on Haunted Hill.

"It would be terrible if someone actually did die," Castle remarked, shamelessly adding, "but the publicity would by terrific."

Castle helped promote the film by springing out of a coffin in the theater lobby at the premiere. He got quite a scare himself when he couldn't budge the lid one night. He kicked and screamed until someone finally let him loose. He was still shaking, leaning against the wall when he was accosted by the wife of one of the local film critics who berated him for making such an awful picture. In his defense,

(Opposite) *Writer Robb White and producer William Castle on the set of* House on Haunted Hill, *(Allied Artists, 1958).*

Castle told the woman that he needed to make money. "This is what the public wants," Castle said, a remark that begs explanation. Castle promised her that when he made more money he'd make better pictures.

Working with White in the little office they shared on the ZIV lot, an office just big enough for a filing cabinet, a desk and two chairs, Castle developed another gimmick. He wanted White to write a haunted house movie with a sequence where a skeleton walks out of an acid bath. How it got there was up to White. All that Castle wanted was the skeleton for what came to be known as Emergo, a new miracle process that caused objects to leap off the motion picture screen without the need for 3-D glasses. The film was *House on Haunted Hill* (1959). Allied Artists gave Castle $200,000 to make it. It turned out to be a bigger success than *Macabre*.

A demonstration of Emergo was given to the folks on the ZIV lot. Sam Goldwyn happened to drop by. His studio was right across the street. Goldwyn was not impressed when Castle's luminous skeleton came wobbling and squeaking from its concealed box at the top of the screen. Nor was he happy when the skeleton fell on his head.

Public screenings were equally hazardous. Once the word leaked out what Emergo was children came to screenings armed with weapons to shoot the skeleton down. Castle didn't care so long as they were coming. The enterprising manager of a New Orleans theater saw how well Castle was doing and modified the carny-type stunt for an engagement of *The Bat* (1959), hoping to break the slump in attendance caused by the end of summer and the children's return to school. The kids turned out in force and Walt Guarino enjoyed the best box office he'd had in months.

The success of *House on Haunted Hill* established Castle's credibility as a money maker. Columbia, a studio that had refused Castle's request to produce, welcomed his return. The first picture that he and White made for the studio was *The Tingler* (1959), Castle's most successful attempt to integrate the audience with the movie. He called it Percepto.

White's scenario was his most bizarre fantasy, about a creature that grows from the human spine during moments of intense fear and only by screaming can the creature be kept in check. As one might expect,

(Opposite) *Patricia Cutts, Judith Evelyn, Philip Coolidge and Vincent Price between scenes in William Castle's* The Tingler *(Columbia, 1959).*

***Castle directs Vincent Price and Patricia Cutts in* The Tingler.**

there's a character in White's scenario who doesn't scream; the creature snaps her spine and winds up causing trouble in a movie theater. And this is when the theater on screen and the real theater converge. The film runs out and the shadow of the Tingler creeps across the blank screen. Vincent Price warns that the only way to stop the monster is to scream. That's the signal to the projectionist to throw the switch. Under ten or twelve seats were some electric motors, war surplus things that Castle got a bargain on. The motors vibrated the seat, in the hope of scaring a scream out of someone. Just in case it didn't Castle planted someone in the audience to get the screams rolling.

"It failed to arouse the customer seated in front of this viewer

Ad art. For The Tingler *(Columbia, 1959) Castle installed little motors to the bottom of a dozen or so theatre seats and turned them on during appropriate moments in the film.*

yesterday, a fearless lad who was sound asleep snoring," wrote Howard Thompson in *The New York Times*. The critic urged Castle to forget about the gimmicks and concentrate on keeping people awake.

It certainly did the trick for a group of elderly women in the San Fernando Valley, the victims of a bored projectionist who decided to test Percepto during an afternoon screening of *The Nun's Story* (1959).

Castle himself purportedly surprised a visitor to his office with one of his silly motors. The man bolted out of his chair and warned Castle that he'd punch him in the nose if he tried it again.

Over the years the accounts of Percepto have been highly exaggerated, probably by Castle himself, to the point where he was believed to have wired seats for electric shock. That would have certainly complied with Howard Thompson's request.

White wrote a cat into his script for *The Tingler*, which caused Castle some displeasure. According to White the animal cost—between trainers and the folks from the ASPCA—around $5,500. And $1,000 every time someone stepped on the cat's tail which White was convinced the cat was trained to make happen as often as possible. Probably just to be obstinate, he wrote an even bigger cat into their next project, *13 Ghosts* (1960). The lion called for in White's script was not the mangy, toothless old thing they wound up with, the one that emptied its bladder the first time it stepped in front of the camera. The incident strengthened Castle's resolve to keep animals out of his pictures.

After *Macabre* several producers used Castle's insurance gimmick in various forms. With the release of *The Screaming Skull* (1958), American International promised to pick up the tab for people who dropped dead during the picture; 20th Century–Fox wanted people to release them of all responsibility for death by fright for their horror combination, *The Horror of Party Beach* and *The Curse of the Living Corpse* (1964). One triple bill offered psychiatric treatment to members of the audience who became emotionally disturbed. Couldn't've hurt. Likewise, after Castle made good his claim that the Tingler would break loose in theaters across the country, American International promised that the title character of *The Amazing Transparent Man* (1959) would invisibly attend every performance and who was to say otherwise?

By the time Castle finished *13 Ghosts*, he'd made a name for himself amongst devotees of horror films, a genre which hadn't then blossomed into what it became in the 1980s. Castle used his notoriety to his advan-

Screaming Skull *borrowed William Castle's life insurance gimmick without bothering to contact an insurance company (American International, 1958).*

tage by enlisting his fans to help sell his product. Don Glut, now a well-known film industry author and lecturer, was coerced into participating in one of Castle's stunts. He rode around with twelve lads, dressed in monster masks, on the back of a truck. Out of a loud speaker droned the voice of Bill Castle, again and again with the same question, "Do you believe in ghosts? I do. And so will you when you see my new picture."

"I don't know how they got my name," Don Glut said, "unless maybe Forry Ackerman gave Columbia a list of names of the people who'd written to his magazine."

Ackerman was the editor-in-chief of a magazine that catered to the horror and science fiction movie phenomenon of the 1950s and '60s, *Famous Monsters of Filmland.* More than anyone else in those days, Ackerman was responsible for uniting a group of fans who had previously thought they were alone in their appetite for the bizarre. It was only natural for Ackerman to be instrumental in bringing the fans and the filmmakers together.

Glut was invited to a "press conference" in one of Chicago's downtown hotels. He stepped into a room where Castle was already in command, looking like Lee J. Cobb with a cigar, Glut's image of the typical Hollywood producer.

SPECIAL SHOCK INSURANCE

After a recent screening of their new triple-terror bill, ORGY OF THE LIVING DEAD, the producers, Europix-International, Ltd., received reports that one movie-goer, as a direct result of viewing this avalanche of grisly horror, had gone insane and been placed in a mental institution. Concerned over this tragic event, the producer, has instituted an unprecedented protection program for future audiences:

I.

THEY ARE INSURING THE SANITY OF EVERY PATRON WHO ENTERS THE THEATRE.

II.

ANYONE WHO LOSES HIS MIND AS A DIRECT RESULT OF VIEWING 'ORGY OF THE LIVING DEAD' WILL RECEIVE FREE PSYCHIATRIC CARE, OR BE PLACED, AT THE PRODUCERS' EXPENSE IN AN ASYLUM FOR THE RE-MAINDER OF HIS NATURAL LIFE!

III.

We regret to inform you, however, that you are not eligible, under the terms of this policy, if you suffer from a nervous condition or any psychiatric problem which can be activated by exposure to fear, shock and horror.

IMPORTANT: This policy-protection plan has been implemented to provide the most complete shock-insurance available to our patrons.

YOU HAVE NOTHING TO LOSE BUT YOUR MIND!

SAID COVERAGE VALID ONLY WHILE VIEWING THIS GHASTLY PROGRAM:

ORGY OF THE LIVING DEAD PG
INCLUDING

1st Hit Mario Bava's   2nd Hit

Curse of the Living Dead   Revenge of the Living Dead
3rd Hit
Fangs of the Living Dead

ALL 3 FEATURES IN BLOOD CHILLING COLOR

After the success of Castle's Macabre, *producers continued to use variations of his life insurance gimmick.*

"It was like meeting God," Glut remarked. "A Hollywood producer or director were people that really didn't exist. Only I was actually meeting one. He wanted to know what everyone thought of *Psycho* (1960). Had they seen it? Did they like it?"

Castle wanted thirteen people for his monster float. Castle prom-

If you wanted to see any of the 13 Ghosts, *you had to look through the ghost viewer (Columbia, 1960).*

ised them skeletons from *Haunted Hill,* motors from *The Tingler,* anything but cash for parading through the streets. Glut wanted to demonstrate his makeup skills and told them he wouldn't need a mask. But after his putty melted under the hot summer sun Glut donned a mask the following day. He kept lifting it off to show some usherette who had caught his eye that there was a handsome guy underneath but the lady wasn't interested.

The monsters ended up at the Republican Presidential Convention where Richard Nixon was being touted. The group chanted "Nix on Nixon" but to little effect. It seems unnecessary to add that nobody ever got the skeletons or motors that were promised.

The gimmick for *13 Ghosts* was Illusion-O, which required a cardboard viewer with a strip of red and blue cellophane, which gave birth to the idea that it was a 3-D movie. Actually, the "Ghost Viewer" allowed audiences to choose whether they wanted to see the ghosts or not, a newfangled way of closing your eyes. Magenta-colored ghosts were superimposed on blue backgrounds. The red cellophane obliterated the ghosts. The blue highlighted them. If you didn't use the viewer at all you could see the ghosts, but not very clearly.

Castle drifted away from horror fantasies to make psychological shockers, after seeing Hitchcock's *Psycho.* He told the press that he'd always wanted to make pictures like Hitchcock. So he instructed Robb

Glenn Corbett is about to get a surprise from Jean Arless in this scene from Castle's Homicidal *(Columbia, 1961).*

White to pen a tale about a psychotic killer with a dual identity. They called it *Homicidal* (1961).

White claimed he hadn't seen *Psycho* when they started the project and was shocked when he finally caught up with it. The film couldn't help but invite comparison to the picture that had inspired it, which Castle took as flattery.

Hitchcock wanted all ticket sales to stop during the last fifteen minutes of his film. Castle actually interrupted his climax with something he called a "Fright Break." A clock appeared on the screen and ticked off 60 seconds while Castle instructed the more timid

In Castle's Mr. Sardonicus *the audience supposedly decided the fate of the title character though only one ending was ever filmed (Columbia, 1961).*

members of the audience to follow their yellow streaks all the way to the Coward's Corner where their money would "sneerfully" be refunded. It was another "I dare you" ruse that audiences seem to cotton to. Only one afternoon, with Castle sitting in the rear of the auditorium, the entire audience headed for a refund. Castle just about died. It never occurred to him that anyone would actually leave before a climax. He found out the audience had already seen the picture at the previous performance. Castle wanted all of the tickets color coded thereafter. And just to be on the safe side, Castle limited his money back guarantee to people over 16, "to protect patrons of tender years from the psychological dangers of being labelled a coward."

Test runs of *Homicidal* in Ohio and Pennsylvania placed it ahead of Hitchcock's picture by 15 percent. Castle severed his partnership with Robb White, which, according to the writer, had been as shaky as Tingler seats since its inception. White characterized himself as an easy-going guy, the sort that wore shorts and t-shirts to business meetings, a habit that drove Castle nuts. They never saw each other socially. All their script conferences were handled by phone. It had been a marriage of convenience and when it was over it came as a relief to them. White returned to television, contributing heavily to *Perry Mason*.

Mr. Sardonicus (1962) was Castle's last attempt to make the audience a part of the story. Using luminescent drawings of a pointed thumb, the audience was invited to decide the fate of the title character. The movie stopped long enough for Castle to take a thumb count before running the thumbs down ending. Castle figured he knew his audience pretty well.

There were no more gimmicks after that. Castle continued to barnstorm his pictures but with a little more dignity, a little more reserve. But his spirit has lived on.

There was a comedy that claimed 287 *certified* laughs, certified by Sindlinger & Company, Incorporated, at their Research Division in Ridley Park, Pennsylvania. A gag almost as good as Castle's life insurance bit. Certainly Castle, Babb, and M.A. Ripps would have been proud of the producer who recently hid a million bucks and planted clues to its whereabouts in one of his movies. Good gimmick but the producer'd been to the well one too many times. After weighing the guy's track record the public decided the reward wasn't big enough.

But so long as there's a movie being made, there's a new gimmick not far behind.

Three

They'll Talk About Spyros Skouras

I think the fact that he was able to mastermind the exhibitors of the country to switch to CinemaScope was Skouras' greatest moment of triumph. About pictures he couldn't tell a good one from a bad one, but on business manipulations he's a master.

—Darryl Zanuck

The expression "bigger is better" seemed to dominate the 1950s decade and the movies always aim to please and all at once there was a war of the widths to see who had the biggest screen.

I couldn't have been more than six years old when my family went on a rare outing to see *The Robe* (1953), in something called Cinema-Scope. But we hadn't driven 30 miles to Hollywood to see this new-fangled CinemaScope. My folks were very religious and *The Robe* promised to be the next best thing to going to church, which we'd done earlier that morning, as we did *every* Sunday morning. We'd get gussied up to go have our good pastor belittle us for an hour or more. We were

37

all miserable sinners and damn lucky to have a God so forgiving. Frankly, God really had no business being anything but forgiving. He was the one in charge. If He didn't like what was going on He should have done something about it, not force people to sit on hard wooden seats and listen to someone whine about it. *The Robe* was a lot like sitting in church. I can recall nothing of it save the ending which was a gigantic closeup of Richard Burton and Jean Simmons, both as tall as the Empire State Building, looking as if they would swallow me whole. Never had I seen the likes of CinemaScope.

If you listened to all of the hoopla at the time, you'd have thought 20th Century–Fox had invented CinemaScope, which was two and a half times wider than the image people were used to seeing. It had been developed by Henri Chretien back in 1928 and experiments in wide screen projection went further back still. But there hadn't been a need for it. People seemed happy enough with the standard 1.33 width-to-ratio frame. Ninety million people used to go to the movies every week. In 1946, 20th Century–Fox made a $22 million profit. It was only $4 million in 1951 and it wasn't going to get any better. It was like that over the movie industry. The two major factors that contributed to the decline were the Supreme Court decision that forced the studios out of exhibition coupled with the arrival of television.

There's a misperception that in their arrogance and ignorance to prepare for the effect of television the studio moguls got precisely what they deserved. Like Goliath when he saw David coming, they hadn't done their homework. But that's not what happened at all. The studios not only saw television coming, they were prepared to corral and brand it. In 1938 Paramount bought into a corporation that manufactured television equipment. Before long the studio had direct or indirect interests in four United States television stations. And the other major studios were all applying to the Federal Communications Commission for licenses of their own. Simultaneously, the Supreme Court was debating whether or not to allow the studios to own their own theaters as it suggested a monopoly. Owning television stations was just more of the same so the FCC put everything on hold until the court ruled. And when the studios were ordered to sell their theaters the applications were dumped in the trash. A double whammy.

The studios collectively staggered into the new decade in a state of shock, headed toward bankruptcy. It was like telling McDonald's they could make burgers but not sell them. In bitter retaliation the

Richard Burton and Jean Simmons filled the giant CinemaScope screen in **The Robe** *(20th Century–Fox, 1953).*

movies started taking potshots at television. In *All About Eve* (1950) Marilyn Monroe asked George Saunders if television had auditions and he glibly assured her that television was nothing but auditions. But it was a wild punch. The situation dictated a more sober approach. If the studios were to compete with television it had to be with action not childish aspersions. The president of 20th Century–Fox, Spyros Skouras, believed the studios had to emphasize the advantages of movies over television. The entertainment may not have been free but it was better dressed. And the screen was bigger. But maybe it wasn't big enough.

Polyvision was the name of the 3-strip system used in Napoleon to achieve the wide screen look that came to be known as Cinerama.

Way back then, when people were experimenting with the size of the screen, Abel Gance used a three-strip system he called Polyvision to make his epic spectacle, *Napoleon*. Raoul Gromoin-Sanson elaborated a bit by adding seven more projectors and a circular screen which he dubbed Cineorama, a demonstration of which was shown at the 1900 world's exposition in Paris. But the most practical of the bunch was Henri Chretien who achieved a wider image with an anamorphic lens which first crammed an image on a single strip of film, then stretched it during projection. The image wasn't as wide as Gromoin-Sanson's but economically it made a lot more sense. It eliminated the need for multiple film strips and projectors and the problem of keeping those projectors in synch. But it was Gance's Polyvision, updated by Fred Waller at Paramount, that Spyros Skouras saw in 1949 and wanted to buy. He was advised not to by the studio's Research and Development Unit. Cinerama, as Waller called his three-projector system, had too many problems. Producers Lowell Thomas and Merian C. Cooper didn't agree and made a feature-length travelog called *This Is Cinerama* (1952). The movie made front page news. Cinerama's larger and curved screen approximated the peripheries of human sight if you sat in the first five rows from the screen. The roller coaster ride, which put the spectators in the front car, sent the more sensitive viewers reeling into the lobby. It played 122 weeks at the Warner Theater in New York and grossed over $4 million. But the cost of converting a theater to play Cinerama was prohibitive and the film only played in five other theaters.* Skouras hadn't gotten such bad advice after all.

Since cost seemed to be the key factor in stopping Skouras from enlarging screen size he told the head of R&D, Earl Sponable, to come up with a low budget Cinerama. The Frenchman Chretien already had the solution. But Paramount had taken an option on it back in 1935. When it lapsed in 1952 Skouras was right there to snap it up.

Skouras boldly announced, before the R&D unit had an opportunity to test Chretien's invention for possible hang-ups, that all Fox releases would be photographed in CinemaScope. Later he was told there was a distortion problem, most evident when the camera or the performers were in motion. A memo went out to all of the cameramen and directors, ordering them to avoid movement whenever possible.

The Music Hall in Detroit, the Boyd in Philadelphia, the Palace in Chicago, the Warner in Washington, D.C., and the Warner in Hollywood, California.

Theater audience is suddenly placed in the front car of a roller coaster in **This Is Cinerama,** *a sequence that had many moviegoers catching their breath in the lobby.*

It was like the old days when sound movies first began and all of the performers had to huddle around the concealed microphone, with the camera confined to a soundproof box.

But Skouras was certain the lens would eventually be perfected. His concern was with selling it to exhibitors and to the public. In that respect Skouras was to wide screen what Elvis Presley was to rock and roll music. At an Allied State Association convention, Skouras told a roomful of delegates that Fox was going to do everything it could to save the industry. He posed as a benevolent protector and anyone who opposed him was being "unfair and injurious" to everyone whose survival depended on the motion picture business. Skouras hit them and hit them hard, like a preacher in his pulpit. He had to. He wasn't just selling CinemaScope, he was selling a package. An expensive package to both producers and exhibitors.

Skouras had to sell CinemaScope to the public the same way studios sold their performers. CinemaScope had to be a star because Fox not only wanted $25,000 per picture to license it, they also insisted on script approval and that all Scope films be in color and stereo sound. Fox also owned the companies that manufactured the new screens and the stereophonic sound equipment. When a couple of the conventioneers suggested Fox might have the makings of a monopoly, Skouras sidestepped the issue, insisting that his company had been forced to make certain investments to encourage various manufacturers to produce the products. Skouras stressed how committed Fox was and the sacrifices that had been made.

Jack Warner wasn't impressed. He told the press that his company would use the newly heralded 3-D instead. Exhibitors were stuck in the middle. Should they convert their theaters to play 3-D or Cinema-Scope? Or just close their doors and go home and watch television with their families? Some of the smaller houses complained that CinemaScope seemed to be geared for spectacles, an impression Skouras fostered when he remarked that the process demanded bigger stories and more action. To the guys with the little screens spectacle didn't mean so much. Worse, if Hollywood was going to make more expensive pictures that probably meant they'd be making fewer pictures, which was hell on the small town exhibitor who had to change his program two or three times a week.

Skouras pressed on. CinemaScope, like castor oil, was for everyone's own good.

The Robe opened at Grauman's (it was still called Grauman's then and I resent the Mann theater chain's bumping his name so they could call it Mann's) Chinese Theatre. It set a record high—$80,000. Sol Schwartz, the president of RKO theaters, wrote a letter to Skouras, applauding CinemaScope as the miracle that would open "wonderful new vistas for the motion picture industry." The owner of a theater in Detroit was so taken with it he threw out his newly purchased 3-D equipment—but then wondered if he hadn't been a little carried away, expressing his doubts to the *Detroit Free Press*: "*The Robe* would have done just as good business if it were not in CinemaScope," he remarked. "CinemaScope just made a great picture better."

Mrs. Dean Gray Edwards, chairwoman of the motion picture division of the General Federation of Women's Clubs, concurred that it was a great picture and presented Skouras with a scroll in recognition of his "distinguished contribution" to the industry. Likewise, the *Christian Herald* honored Skouras, only they did it with a plaque, in appreciation for his company's "outstanding contribution to religious drama." Meanwhile, Skouras was counting the box office contributions. In its first two weeks at New York's Roxy Theatre, *The Robe* did a breathtaking $578,427. And so it went at practically every theater in every city. Fox's next Scope feature, *How to Marry a Millionaire* (1953), opened at the

Audiences flocked to see the first CinemaScope film The Robe.

Fox Wilshire Theater in Hollywood to a sell-out audience. Opening night was one of those events that almost never happens anymore, when celebrities turned out by the dozens. Among the people in attendance that night were Charles Brackett, Robert Mitchum, Lauren Bacall, Cecil B. DeMille, Bing Crosby, Humphrey Bogart, Susan Hayward, the producer-writer Nunnally Johnson, and the star, Marilyn Monroe.

"Marilyn Monroe will have to lie down before the audience can get a look at her," one filmmaker remarked, a not so kind reference to the oblong look of CinemaScope, which director George Stevens felt put "a boa constrictor to better advantage than a man." Cinematographer Leo Shamroy said "it wrecked the art of film for a decade." None of which had any effect on *How to Marry a Millionaire's* take, which was something like 7 million the first year. Other CinemaScope projects were reported in the works:

The Queen of Sheba—based on the biblical book of Solomon.

Prince Valiant—a dramatization of the adventure newspaper serial.

Twelve Mile Reef—an unusual drama of human conflict set against the colorful sponge-fishing coast of Florida, filmed entirely off Key West and in the Bahamas. Produced by Raymond Klune and Robert Bassler, directed by Robert D. Webb with a cast including Terry Moore, Robert Wagner, Gilbert Roland.

The Gun and the Cross—from a novel by Isabelle Gibson Ziegler.

Sir Walter Raleigh—a stirring story of the celebrated Englishman.

The Racer—to be filmed in Italy during the Gold Cup races.

Prince of Players—Eleanor Ruggles' Book-of-the-Month biography of the fabulous Edwin Booth.

King of the Khyber Rifles—an adaptation of Talbot Mundy's novel.

The Wandering Jew—the world-famous play by E. Temple Thurston.

Irving Berlin's There's No Business Like Show Business—a smash musical with a great cast.

Hell and High Water—exciting story of a mission to destroy a secret enemy air installation in Korea.

The Story of Demetrius—carrying forward the life and adventures of the focal slave character created in *The Robe*.

The Story of Jezebel—from the Old Testament book of Kings, a dramatic and sultry tale.

The Egyptian—a Darryl F. Zanuck production, based on the best-selling novel by Mika Waltari.

Marilyn Monroe wowed 'em in Fox's CinemaScope production How to Marry a Millionaire *(1953).*

A promotion tour (described as a "ballyhoo wagon") for The Egyptian *(20th Century–Fox, 1954).*

Many of the projects fizzled, as they often do, but *The Egyptian* (1954) definitely made it with a tremendous campaign to back it. Thirty-five hundred billboards heralded the coming of it in every major city, on every main artery where the space could be bought. Producer Zanuck was featured on Ed Sullivan's "Toast of the Town" and Edward R. Murrow's "See It Now" television shows. An article written by Zanuck (or the studio's publicity department) appeared in newspapers across the country. "As soon as I read Mika Waltari's best-selling novel, I knew that it had to be made into a motion picture, and then for two years after that I puzzled over how to do the book justice," wrote Zanuck. "The day I saw the first tests in CinemaScope and color by De Luxe, I knew that I had my answer. The new screen process would provide the depth of feeling and the impact necessary to transmit to audiences the meaning and social significance of Waltari's book."

M-G-M wanted to use CinemaScope for their version of the Broadway musical *Kiss Me Kate* (1953), but Chretien couldn't supply the

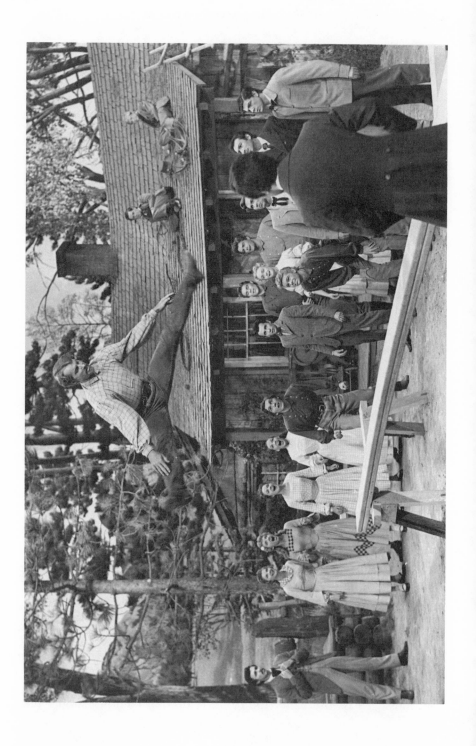

lenses on time so the studio made it in 3-D instead. Skouras made sure that wouldn't happen again by giving the account to Bausch and Lomb. When M-G-M made *Knights of the Round Table* (1953) the scope lenses were on hand. The picture won *Boxoffice* magazine's Blue Ribbon Award for the best family picture that month and was generally well-received. The president of the Motion Picture Council for Brooklyn, Mrs. George H. Sutcliffe (she could have a title but not her own name) applauded the movie's "gorgeous pageantry and fine spiritual and in-spirational quality," while Mrs. E.F. Carran, who belonged to the Cleveland branch of the council, exclaimed that you simply had to see it to appreciate the way it was "so vividly done with CinemaScope." One enthusiastic Chattanooga reviewer said that chivalry in CinemaScope was "better than volumes of words!" It was music to Skouras's ears to say nothing of the folks at M-G-M. Yet, when the same studio made *Seven Brides for Seven Brothers* (1954), a musical loosely based on Stephen Vincent Benét's *The Sobbin' Women*, two versions were shot — one in Scope, the other flat.* Either they were afraid the process was a passing fad or they were concerned about all of the theaters that couldn't afford the $20,000 it took to convert to Scope. The studio had waited five years for the option on the story to lapse so they could make the picture. They weren't about to take any chances.

Warner Brothers resisted the move to Scope for as long as it could, first by riding with 3-D and, when that proved to be a mistake, by developing a system of their own, identical to Chretien's lens, which in-cluded its defects. By 1954, Bausch and Lomb had pretty much ironed out the problems. Winfield Andrus, reporting in *Film Daily*, told her readers that fuzzy backgrounds were a thing of the past. "No longer do the viewers' eyes feel strain as the camera pans across a wide vista, nor are the side portions of the projected image distorted." Bowing to technical superiority, and to the fact that the name CinemaScope, as Skouras fought to promote, had become a major selling factor. The studio finally gave up on its WarnerSuperScope and signed with Fox. "We are adopting CinemaScope in an effort to clarify and standardize

(Opposite) *One of the finest dance numbers ever pictured here in this scene from* Seven Brides for Seven Brothers. *The movie was released in both flat and CinemaScope versions (M-G-M, 1954).*

*Apparently, the folks at M-G-M aren't aware of this alternate flat version. Unnecessary and costly "scanned–Scope" versions were sold to television and video tape.

for exhibitors and the public a single process, thus eliminating any possibility of confusion," a studio spokesman told the press, as if Warners gave a fig about that. Skouras said he was "inspired."

The Command (1954) was Warners' first Scope release and the advertisements made the most of it. The name CinemaScope was the biggest thing on the poster besides the title, larger than any of the performers or the people who made it. And several newspapers ran the following: "Filmed in WarnerColor, Warner Bros., the first major studio that embraced 3-D with the thriller, 'House of Wax,' went into the wide open spaces in country never before filmed on such a scale to bring this sweeping tale of a band of fighting soldiers on a mission in the West. With action as a background for the story, and panoramic views of beautiful country as its backdrop, 'The Command' becomes something to wait for on local moviegoers' schedules.

"Using the CinemaScope anamorphic lens, which literally sees and records each scene in nearly as broad a scope as human vision, 'The Command' is the first CinemaScope for Warner Bros., who have announced plans for the filming of many more stories in the new medium. According to Jack L. Warner, studio production chief, Warner Bros. will film in CinemaScope those stories which by the nature of their settings and dramatic proportions best lend themselves to the eye-filling magnitude of CinemaScope."

Cue magazine described *The Command* as the "kind of picture CinemaScope was made for" while *The Motion Picture Daily* was a bit less vague: "A rip-roaring story of the American Frontier.... Should make out handsomely at the box-office. Exhibitors who do not show this in CinemaScope are selling themselves short." *Film Daily* concurred: "CinemaScope does special things for *The Command*. The Western takes on a new and impressive aspect. Constantly exciting and sharpened to a fine edge for fuller impact by the sweeping photography!" That was all Walt Disney needed to hear. Disney was looking to get into live action features since the cost of feature-length cartoons was prohibitive, and for his premiere entry in the United States, Jules Verne's *20,000 Leagues Under the Sea* (1954), he wanted to go first class. But Disney ran into trouble with the anamorphic process. It didn't allow enough light to photograph the miniature submarine. The talented and inventive Harper Goff came up with the solution. Another submarine was built squashed and photographed with a regular lens. When the image was stretched by the anamorphic lens it looked normal.

The Command *was the first CinemaScope release from Warner Brothers. As you can see the advertisement made the most of it.*

Howard Hughes had RKO develop its own anamorphic process, SuperScope, offered at a bargain rate. It became the darling of the low budget producer. The newly formed American Releasing Corporation had to pay only $3,000 for the process. Even if ARC would or could have afforded CinemaScope, Fox would never have approved the project.

This is the original "Underwater!" scene
as it was photographed in the usual way.

This is the same "Underwater!" scene after
its anamorphic "squeeze print" processing.

This is the same scene from Howard Hughes' "Underwater!" as it appears after the new
Superscope process, on the wide screen, with greater clarity, depth and real-life in-
timacy. Jane Russell, Gilbert Roland, Richard Egan and Lori Nelson are co-starred in this
Technicolor production, which took three years to make and cost RKO Radio $3,000,000.

SuperScope, the poor man's CinemaScope. Pictured here—Lori Nelson, Gilbert Roland, Jane Russell, and Richard Egan in Underwater *(RKO, 1955).*

SuperScope required an anamorphic lens during projection but not during the filming. Photographers had to be mindful to keep the action away from the top and bottom of the frame because the image was masked to give it a more rectangular look then squeezed during the printing. The image was not as wide as actual scope and because of the loss of negative area was much grainier although it wasn't distorted like real Scope.* But the more imaginative producers realized they could achieve the same effect by simply cropping the top of the frame, giving

For television prints the original unmasked negative is used, eliminating the need to scan the print. And for that reason SuperScope films show better on television.

When Walt Disney realized his feature-length cartoons were becoming too ex-
pensive to produce he went all out for his first big live action feature by adding
CinemaScope to it (from 20,000 Leagues Under the Sea, *Buena Vista, 1954).*

birth to the now standard aspect ratio of 1.85 to 1. This nonanamorphic
effect was called just about anything anybody felt like calling it: Ter-
rorscope (*The Beast with 1,000,000 Eyes*, 1956), Wide Vision (*Teenage
Doll*, 1957), Horrorscope (*The Beginning of the End*, 1957), Naturama
(*Juvenile Jungle*, 1958), Ultrascope (*The Dead One*, 1961), and so on.

SuperScope died with RKO in 1957 and never posed a real threat
to CinemaScope. Only VistaVision, a wide screen process developed by
Paramount, gave Skouras a few anxious moments and not because the
image was better than his CinemaScope, which it was, but because of
its sound system, which employed a single optical track that would play
on a conventional single speaker through an integrator that simulated
stereo. The wider image was achieved by running a regular 35mm
negative through a camera horizontally. It was corrected during printing so it could be projected the traditional way, leaving slightly more
space between frames to compensate for the wider image. This in-

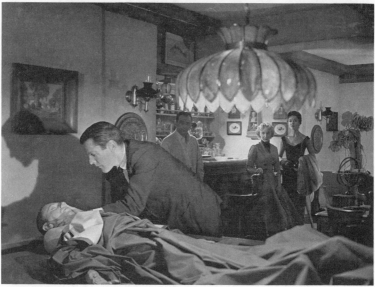

SuperScope was RKO's answer to CinemaScope, a wide screen technique that was a lot easier on the budget. (Top) Peggy Castle in Oklahoma Woman *(American Releasing Corp., 1956). (Bottom) Kevin McCarthy, King Donovan, Carolyn Jones, and Dana Wynter from the classic* Invasion of the Body Snatchers *(Allied Artists, 1956).*

creased the picture's clarity tremendously. Paramount called it "motion picture high fidelity" and indeed it was.

As there was a rising opposition to Fox's coupling Scope to stereo sound, VistaVision seemed like a terrific alternative. The owners of small theaters knew it was pointless to wire their places for stereo. The effect would be negligible. Drive-in theatre owners agreed and were adamant about expressing their feelings. During a meeting of the National Allied Drive-In Theaters Association one angry fellow cried, "Let's tell Mr. Skouras we are not going to tear up up our pavements and rewire our ramps for such an asinine sound system for drive-ins." But Fox had invested too much money to scrap it so Skouras kept stalling until all the major studios started drifting toward VistaVision. Skouras buckled. He announced that all Fox films would be available in four-track magnetic sound, single-track magnetic sound, or single-track optical sound. VistaVision fell by the wayside.

Toward the middle of 1955 Fox tried to improve the clarity of Scope by shooting in 55mm for reduction to a standard 35mm format. It was an improvement but not one that people seemed to notice so after only two features, *Carousel* and *The King and I* (both 1956), CinemaScope 55 was discontinued, eclipsed by Todd A-O which used a 65mm negative for a 70mm positive, leaving room for the soundtrack. The image it created was brighter and sharper than anything before it, especially when projected at 30 frames a second as originally intended.

Todd A-O was the creation of Mike Todd, the man who made front page headlines in 1957 with his marriage to Elizabeth Taylor and again the following year with his death in a plan crash. His real name was Avram Goldenbogen, one of the original partners in Cinerama.

There were some other anamorphic wide screen processes: TohoScope (*Mothra*, 1962), RegalScope (*Kronos*, 1957), Techniscope (*A Fistful of Dollars*, 1964), and others. But the one that blew them all out of the water was Panavision. Panavision arrived on the scene in 1957 in M-G-M-'s *Raintree County* and it was clearly a superior format. It took ten years for Fox to admit they'd been bettered and by that time Spyros Skouras wasn't in charge of things at the studio anymore. The man who almost singlehandedly made wide screen a reality suffered a power loss in the wake of the studio's biggest financial disaster, *Cleopatra* (1963), which nearly drove the studio into bankruptcy.

UltraPanavision eventually replaced Cinerama which was then being used for something other than travelogues. George Pal's *The*

There were only two features shot in CinemaScope 55—Carousel (above) and The King and I *(below). Although it was superior to regular CinemaScope audiences didn't seem to notice the difference (both 20th Century–Fox, 1956).*

The first Cinerama movie with a plot: **The Wonderful World of the Brothers Grimm** *(M-G-M; 1962).*

Wonderful World of the Brothers Grimm (1962) was the first Cinerama movie with a plot and it was followed by the spectacular *How the West Was Won* (1963). But the three images never quite blended properly and everything looked like it was shot through a fishbowl. UltraPanavision eliminated all that. Yet there didn't seem to be much call for it. Most people didn't know the difference between Cinerama and CinemaScope. In fact, they didn't know the difference between scope and 1:85, partly because most theaters never had a screen wide enough to accommodate the full scope image. As the size of the screens shrank to fit the matchboxes that people now know as theaters the importance of Panavision has pretty well been nullified. There's every reason to suspect that it'll have a resurgence with the advent of wide screen television. And you can be sure the old CinemaScope movies'll show up again. They might even make a to-do over *The Robe.* And maybe, if someone does their homework, they'll talk about Spyros Skouras, the guy who started it all. In a manner of speaking, of course.

Four

It Comes Right at You

"We'll throw things at the public until they start throwing them back."
—*Jerry Wald*, **Motion Picture Producer**

It was May of 1951. A group of studio executives and members of the press were gathered together in a small rental studio in Culver City to see a demonstration of something called Natural Vision. The host of the affair was Milton L. Gunzburg, once described by *Time* magazine as "a mild little man." He'd written for radio and motion pictures (*Sister Kenny*, 1946 and *Big Town*, 1947) but turned his attention to 3-D photography, convinced that it was the solution to Hollywood's revenue slump. What the people saw that afternoon was a collection of scenes of California hot rods photographed in Gunzburg's 3-D process. No one in the room shared Gunzburg's enthusiasm or his belief in the process. There were a few polite if condescending remarks. The studio cleared in record time and mild little Gunzburg left for home.

The reaction was the same everywhere Gunzburg went—until John Arnold saw Natural Vision. Arnold was the chief of the camera department at M-G-M. It looked like Gunzburg had finally hit pay dirt but the studio let the option lapse a few months later and Gunzburg was right back where he started, slightly the worse for wear. Then Arch Oboler, who'd recently made the transition from radio to motion pictures, saw Natural Vision and thought it was terrific.

Oboler was best known for his horror radio show "Lights Out" and his penchant for the bizarre carried over into his movies so it was hardly unusual that 3-D appealed to him. That he chose to make an action-adventure film in the medium instead of something with a supernatural flavor is a little peculiar but it was *The Lions of Zulu* that went before the stereoscopic cameras on June 20, 1952, a title that was eventually changed to *Bwana Devil* (1953). It premiered at the Hollywood and Downtown Paramount theaters in California on Thanksgiving Eve without benefit of a distributor, and in the first week the take was $154,000.

United Artists stepped in and bought *Bwana Devil* for $500,000 after the first half million. Two months later, despite the critical lambasting given the movie in practically every newspaper in the country, it grossed over $400,000 at 30 theaters. At New York's Loew's State theater alone it earned $79,000 in two weeks. The smell of money caught Hollywood's attention in a way that Gunzburg's demonstration reel never could have but still there was the fear that the novelty would be short-lived.

Fox's Darryl Zanuck openly declared that any process that required the use of glasses was bound to fail. Furthermore, Zanuck thought the whole idea was absurd. "I have been supplying my own third dimension all my life," he chortled. "What we need is to open up, open up wide."

Of course Zanuck and 20th Century–Fox had already committed themselves to CinemaScope so his opinion was hardly an unbiased one and one that wasn't shared by Bob O'Donnell, an exhibitor who owned the largest string of theaters in Texas. O'Donnell, believed by many to be one of the industry's greatest showmen, responded to Zanuck's self-serving jab by pointing out that only a handful of his patrons had complained about the glasses. He admitted that there had been a number of complaints about the quality of the picture itself but no more than usual.

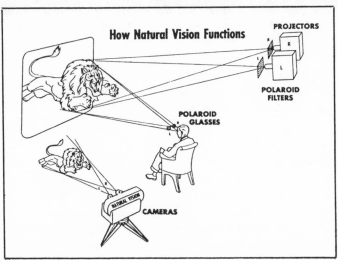

(Above) *Milt Gunzburg made a small fortune selling his polaroid 3-D glasses to audiences hungry for 3-D thrills. The glasses cost 6.7 cents to make. Gunzburg sold them for 10 cents. (Below) Illustration of 3-D in action. Two slightly different images of the same subject are projected onto a screen. Polaroid light filters are placed in front of the two projectors. The two images are superimposed on top of each other. Polaroid glasses worn by audiences correct the image.*

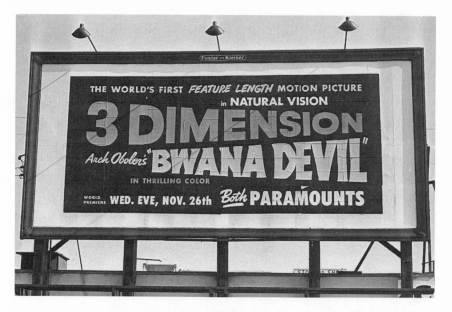

Nobody was interested in 3-D until the independently made Bwana Devil *(United Artists, 1953) made a pot of money. This 24-sheet poster was designed to attract the attention of the passing motorist.*

Bwana Devil has often been referred to as the first 3-D feature, possibly because it was advertised as the first feature in Natural Vision. Actually, the first 3-D feature was made in Italy in 1937 and the very first 3-D films go all the way back to 1915 when Edwin S. Porter and William E. Waddell publicly screened their "anaglyphic" footage of New York and New Jersey at the Astor Theater in New York.

Experiments in 3-D date back to ancient Egypt when drawings were made, side by side, with slight horizontal differences. When viewed through a stereoscope the drawings appeared to have depth. These drawings, called stereographs, were similar to anaglyphs, which were also two separate drawings, one in red and the other green or blue. To achieve the dimensional effect red and blue (or green) filters were used. In both cases each eye sees a slightly different view of the same object which the brain fuses together.

Milt Gunzburg borrowed from all that had gone before him and added a few refinements. For his Natural Vision two film strips, one for the left and one for the right eye, are exposed simultaneously which means twice the amount of film is required for 3-D movies. And two projectors, in perfect synchronization, were needed to run them. Nowadays an entire feature is mounted on one gigantic reel but thirty years ago movies were mounted on reels that contained about twenty minutes of movie. At the end of each reel a circle at the top righthand corner of the frame would cue the operator to switch projectors. 3-D movies were mounted on 40-minute reels but since both projectors were in operation all of the early 3-D movies required an intermission. (Which is also why most 3-D features were no longer than 80 or 90 minutes.) If the film broke the operator had two choices: replace the number of frames affected with black film or remove the same number of frames from the other reel. To make this task a little easier most 3-D films had edge markings that identified the reel number, footage count, and whether it was a left or right reel.

After the success of *Bwana Devil* producers started tripping over each other to rush their own 3-D films into theaters before the public lost interest. Warner Bros. assumed they'd get the drop on everyone with their *House of Wax* (1953), a remake of their own early Technicolor horror film *Mystery of the Wax Museum* (1933). The Grand Guignol tale about a madman who uses corpses dipped in wax to populate his museum seemed like an ideal subject for the sensational new film process. Milt Gunzburg brought his camera to the studio where it was carried from set to set in a padlocked trunk, guarded whenever it wasn't in use.

Meanwhile, over at Universal-International, producer William Alland was secretly making his own 3-D feature, a science fiction drama titled *It Came from Outer Space* (1953). "Jack Arnold was directing it," said the film's star, Richard Carlson, "and he said: 'You know the secret about this 3-D is that we're trying to beat Warner's *House of Wax*.'" Of course their cover would have been blown if they'd hired Milt Gunzburg so U-I's resident cameraman, Clifford Stine, was ordered to develop a 3-D camera of his own.

As it turned out the subterfuge was for nothing. Columbia got the drop on them both by quickly revamping a project that was already in the works and completing it in a brisk eleven days. *Man in the Dark* (1953), according to one enthusiastic (and misguided) critic, contained "enough of the startle-'em trick photography gimmicks to more than satisfy the novelty seekers." The owner of a Colorado theater thought differently. "Didn't make anything, not even the overhead," he grumbled. The film's much heralded "wild roller coaster ride" was

Vincent Price looks on as Phyllis Kirk receives instructions from director Andre de Toth in this behind-the-scenes look at the making of House of Wax *(Warner Bros., 1953).*

accomplished by plopping a handful of uninspired extras in a dummy car in front of a back projection screen. The effect would have been iffy at best but since the footage projected on the screen was 2-D the scam became even more obvious. The film did contain one memorable line of dialog, spoken by leading lady Audrey Totter. "When you're in love," she helpfully tells her co-star, Edmond O'Brien, "a quarter's just two dimes and a nickel."

By contrast, Warner's *House of Wax* was a four star masterpiece. It was lavishly produced with deep sets taking full advantage of the 3-D effect. Unlike Columbia's effort it was in color. There had been some concern that Andre de Toth may not have been an ideal choice for director since he only had one eye and therefore couldn't see depth but then Beethoven couldn't hear music and it didn't cramp his style. *Box-*

Perhaps the most famous of all 3-D shockers, House of Wax *was a remake of the* 1933 Mystery of the Wax Museum *(Warner Bros., 1953).*

Anyone who ever saw House of Wax *in 3-D remembers the famous paddle ball sequence with Reggie Rymal.*

office thought that de Toth did a splendid job, calling the film "made-to-order for patrons who revel in . . . spine-chilling epics." *The Christian Science Monitor* wasn't nearly as pleased. They complained that while *House of Wax* may have been a three-dimensional movie it had a one-dimensional purpose which was to scare people. "That it succeeds," wrote the *Monitor* in one issue, "is no credit to anyone in particular."

With the film expected to pull in $8 million, Jack Warner gave the order for 22 more 3-D features, only five of which were made.* And while Warner was enjoying the success of his first 3-D venture, the folks at U-I were smiling at the box office receipts from *It Came from*

(Opposite) *Phyllis Kirk is alone in the wax museum. Well, almost. That's Charles Bronson lurking in the background (Warner Bros., 1953).*

Some of the projects originally slated for 3-D were East of Eden, Helen of Troy, The High and the Mighty, Mr. Roberts, *and the Judy Garland version of* A Star Is Born.

Outer Space which had been as cunningly crafted for stereoscopic
effects as *House of Wax*. The very first image the audience is treated to
is a ball of fire streaking across the desert in the night sky. Finally it
lands right on top of the camera, causing an equally camera conscious
landslide.

When the picture premiered at Los Angeles' Pantages Theater, the
rocks actually bounced into the audience. Styrofoam rocks that is, installed above the screen (like Bill Castle's silly skeleton), released at the
height of the avalanche.

The 3-D effects aside, *It Came from Outer Space* had more to offer
its audience than most of the 3-D films that would follow. It was a note
of sanity during a troubled time, when an enemy was simply someone
a little different, a condition that unfortunately hasn't changed so much
in thirty-five years.

Unlike most films about visitations from outer space, the aliens
were friendly and frightened. It was the work of author Ray Bradbury
during his most creative period. His scenario is laced with the sort of
poetic writing that made so many of his novels classics. Although Bradbury is credited with the story only, for all practical purposes what you
see is what he wrote.

Being unfamiliar with what a screen treatment was supposed to be,
roughly a 10- or 20-page outline, Bradbury gave Universal something in
excess of 80 pages, practically a completed script. The writer who is
credited with the screenplay, Harry Essex, pretty much transcribed
Bradbury's treatment into screenplay form, adding a few touches of his
own here and there, usually to the detriment of the original. Essex
denied this in a recent interview.

Essex claimed that Bradbury's treatment was no longer than three
pages, and when confronted with the fact that the interviewer had seen
copies of three full-length treatments with Bradbury's name, Essex
stuck to his story. "Ray's story was a very short piece, and I did the treatment, which was accepted," Essex remarked. "Some time later, when
we were invited to attend the preview, some very formal invitations
were sent out, and there was Ray Bradbury's name above mine. But of
course I could understand what the situation was. I mean, we're talking
about an internationally popular writer, a famous man! There was
enough credit for everybody; the people *inside* the business knew that
I had written the screenplay, and that was all that mattered . . . [Brad-
bury's] not a screenplay writer. But as a matter of fact, it was through

It Came from Outer Space (1953) was the first 3-D feature from Universal International.

It Came from Outer Space that Ray got a very important job, writing *Moby Dick* for John Huston, who probably thought that Ray *had* written the *Outer Space* screenplay. And *Moby Dick* was a fiasco and a disaster. Ray is primarily a novelist and a short story writer, and there's a difference between dramatization and pure narrative writing" (*Fangoria*, Vol. 7, #68, p. 15, article by Tom Weaver).

One has only to examine the career of Harry Essex — *Boston Blackie and the Law, Dangerous Business* (both 1946), *Dragnet, Desperate* (1947), *Bodyguard* and additional dialog for *He Walked by Night* (both 1948), *Wyoming Mail* (1950), *Models Inc.,* and *The Las Vegas Story* (both 1952), *I, the Jury* and *Devil's Canyon* (both 1953), *Southwest Passage* (1954), *Teenage Crime Wave* and *Mad at the World* (both 1955), *Raw Edge* and *Showdown at Abilene* (both 1956), and his swan song, *Octoman* (1971) — to see there is nothing that suggests the eloquence in *It Came from Outer Space.* And when Steven Spielberg credited the film with inspiring his own *Close Encounters of the Third Kind* (1977), it was Bradbury he thanked, not Essex.

Despite the success of both *It Came from Outer Space* and *House of Wax,* there were many people who believed 3-D would die because people had to wear glasses. Jack Warner dismissed those doomsayers as "irresponsible." He reminded a group of exhibitors that there were those who predicted the death of sound movies. And while the debate over the glasses continued, Milt Gunzburg landed an exclusive contract with Polaroid to distribute the cardboard glasses at ten cents apiece. In a few short weeks Polaroid's stock rose 30 percent. *Life* magazine called 3-D the "most frenzied boom since the birth of sound" and by the following month *Film Daily,* one of the trade magazines, began a column called "3-D Bulletin Board."

Cecil B. DeMille postponed the starting date of *The Ten Commandments* (1956), hoping to determine if 3-D was coming or going. Years before, when sound was still a gimmick, DeMille had made the mistake of shooting *The Godless Girl* (1929) as a silent film. He wasn't about to be caught with his pants down again. "One thing matters above all else," he delcared. "If a picture is good, it will have an audience; if not, it won't. Permanent success can't be judged by the successes of the first five or six pictures utilizing any special process because the element of novelty is present."

With considerably less to invest than DeMille anticipated with his biblical spectacle, Columbia was back with *Fort Ti* (1953), directed by our old friend William Castle, a lackluster western set in the time of the French-Indian war, billed as the "first great outdoor epic of America in 3-D!" It was the sort of lethargic and uninspired programmer that came to be the rule rather than the exception in the selection of properties to be lensed in stereovision.

Likewise, M-G-M's cautious entry into the 3-D market, *Arena* (1953), had nothing to recommend it aside from the novelty of depth.

The studio with "more stars than in the heavens" peopled the cast with newcomers Gig Young and Polly Bergen. The *Boxoffice* review pretty much summed it up: "It's an unpretentious vehicle that Mighty Metro chose through which to submerge a venturesome toe into the currently torrid 3-dimension stream. A rodeo story, its plot, situations, dialog and characters are strictly from formula. Resultantly, the feature could never have hoped to transcend mediocrity without the use of the trick photography. But the broncs, Brahmans, buckaroos, and their babes offer flexible and photogenic material for the gimmicks of 3-D, and it seems reasonable to suppose that the film will enjoy the same wide patronage being accorded to others made in that process."

A small town exhibitor in Elmore, Minnesota, felt a lot more kindly toward it: "This was the best received 3-D picture of the five we have played. The rodeo scenes were good, the print was good and it ran off like a charm. If you have 3-D installed and have horse lovers in your town, give this your best time. It will help to put over 3-D in small towns and help take away the bad taste from some of the previous 3-D horror films."

But it wasn't the horror films that put a bad taste in exhibitors' mouths, it was the uncertainty of which gimmick to bet on, 3-D or CinemaScope. "I don't know how the other little exhibitors feel these days, but I'm getting woozy and plenty scared," said exhibitor Ken Corkum in Nova Scotia. "Are we to understand that shortly all films are to be made for 3-D, stereophonic sound, etc.? Does this mean finis to the 2-D feature? How—yes, how—can we hope to pay for all this new equipment? I wish some of the producers would give some sign of assurance that it will be years yet before this becomes necessary or, at least, give us some ray of hope—if there are any rays to give."

One answer came from the Sterling Sales and Service company in the form of an amazing package deal: a 3-D projection system, sound amplification, and an all-purpose screen. And all for the amazing low, low price of only $5,000 "more or less." Robert Hanover, an enterprising inventor in Philadelphia, had an even better offer. According to Hanover, his Photorama system eliminated the need for 3-D glasses by using a screen mounted on a concave frame that presented two concave surfaces to the viewer. The screen and lens surfaces were placed in such a way as to eliminate the outer focus effects inherent on large curved screens. The entire screen was curved about its horizontal axis, and the center portion was curved about its vertical axis. The center portion was surrounded by screen areas that inclined away from the ends, and end portions curved toward the lens, producing the 3-D effect. How? Because of the various parts of the picture that appeared on corresponding portions of the screen, that's how! And according to the company that manufactured and installed these screens, Norpat, exhibitors who'd seen the screens in action at two Philly theaters were so thrilled that the phone had been ringing off the hook with orders ever since. Nevertheless, it would not have been wise to invest in Norpat stock that year.

"Many confusing and conflicting statements have been made recently concerning the technical aspects of three-dimension," warned Bob O'Donnell. "I certainly do not want to add to the confusion but I have been advised by several optical specialists and experts that true and actual three-dimension pictures cannot be achieved without the use of glasses. . . .* During this exciting period of three-dimension and all of its ramifications, no word is more important than flexibility. Let's not try to tell our producers how to make pictures, and let's let the play be the deciding factor. And, if the story lends itself to 2-D, 3-D, CinemaScope, stereophonic sound, wide-screens, etc., let the producer in his good judgement decide the use of the gimmick, if necessary. We do not tell the producer when to use color. The story is still the most imporant thing to consider. Above all else, let's give the public solid entertainment, novel and fresh entertainment" (*Boxoffice*, March, 1954).

Ignoring O'Donnell's request for fresh entertainment, Paramount took a shot at the 3-D market with an adaptation of a Frank Slaughter novel, *Sangaree* (1953), which promised love scenes between Fernando Lamas and Arlene Dahl so sensational and intimate that it simulated the experience of "peeking through a keyhole!" When the film's producer was asked if he was concerned about the public's possible adverse reaction to donning glasses he replied: "They'll wear toilet seats around their necks if you give 'em what they want to see." The picture had been in production for twelve days before the front office decided to shoot it in 3-D. The previous footage was scrapped and $400,000 was added to the budget.

Warners was quick to follow *House of Wax* with *The Charge at Feather River* (1953), starring Guy Madison who'd developed quite a

Boxoffice, Vol. 64, No. 17, p. 35, March 6, 1954.

following with his Wild Bill Hickok television show. Joining the 3-D spree was Allied Artists with *The Maze* (1953), RKO with *Second Chance* (1953), and most surprising of all, 20th Century–Fox who had every reason in the world to hope their own *Inferno* (1953), as well as everyone else's 3-D pictures, would flop.

Milt Gunzburg publicly warned everyone that inferior quality could kill the 3-D industry but when he said it he wasn't referring to content. By May there were no fewer than thirteen reported dimensional systems. The only thing that seemed to be in immediate danger was Gunzburg's monopoly. For the record there were:

1. **Columbia 3-D.** Originally introduced as Vitascope. It was a single camera, utilizing two lenses and two negatives. No mirrors or prisms required.

2. **Depth-O-Vision.** Developed by Triscope Corp. owned by producer Edward Alperson and Howard Anderson.

3. **Dunning 3-D.** Utilized a lightweight, 68-pound single camera developed by Carroll Dunning, offered to producers by Nat LeVine through Dunningcolor Corp. Camera had two lenses, 1.3 inches apart, and held two rolls of negatives. Differed from Natural Vision in that no mirror was utilized. First used on *I, the Jury* (1953).

4. **Lippert 3-D.** Designed by Producers Service, first used on a short subject called *College Capers.*

5. **Natural Vision.** First of the 3-D systems developed by Milton L. Gunzburg's Natural Vision Corporation. Required the use of polarized viewers, two synchronized projectors, polarized filters, large-sized magazines plus a polarized screen or specially approved coating for old screen.

6. **Nord 3-D.** Reportedly designed by a Minneapolis firm as a single-camera, single-projection, 3-D system.

7. **Paravision.** All-purpose name given by Paramount to their 3-D and wide screen productions, though it was soon dropped. Studio reported the development of a panoramic screen which purported to give the illusion of depth to flat films.

8. **Polaroid 3-D.** Developed by Polaroid Company who, at the time, were working on a device called a Vectograph which would print a 3-D image on a single strip of film.

9. **RKO 3-D.** A double-lens camera developed by John Norling, first used in 1933 by M-G-M for short subjects which then required red and green glasses.

10. **Reiger 3-D.** Another system that printed two images on a single strip of film and required red and green glasses. First used on a Lippert short subject, *A Day in the Country*.

11. **Stereo-Cine.** An English system originally called Tri-Opticon, introduced in America by producer Sol Lesser.

12. **True-Stereo 3-D.** Used two cameras with an automatic interlocking control which supposedly insured against faulty synchronization. First used on Astor's *Robot Monster*.

13. **Universal 3-D.** Developed by Clifford Stine, it required two cameras mounted side by side (one upside down). First used on *It Came from Outer Space*.

14. **Warner 3-D.** After using Natural Vision for their first two stereo-vision features, the studio developed their own system which was similar to the one used by Universal. First used on *Hondo*.

15. **Zeiss-Ikon.** German 3-D process acquired by Frank and Maurice King. It used a one-strip film in a standard camera with a prism attached.

The majority of these systems required the use of polarized filters, two projectors, viewers, etc. And if some patrons were unhappy about having to pay an additional ten cents for the classes they had nothing on the exhibitors who had to foot the bill for making their theaters 3-D ready. A new screen could run anywhere from $350 to $750. Paint for an old screen was nine bucks a gallon and it really didn't work very well. Once you added new filters and magazines large enough to hold 40 minutes of film, and had the necessary wiring installed, the exhibitor could look forward to a $2000 or $3000 tab. Chicago's Great States Circuit refused to exhibit films in 3-D. But it didn't slow the stampede any.

Screenwriter Harry Essex, for instance, on the basis of his participation on *It Came from Outer Space*, wangled a deal to direct *I, the Jury* (1953), adapting his screenplay from the novel of the same name by Mickey Spillane. Spillane's novel was the first in a series of highly successful, gritty accounts of detective Mike Hammer, an unpleasant and violent Neanderthal whom Spillane, a former comic book writer, somehow found admirable. Hammer bullied his way through each story, pounding his enemies into jelly and treating his women like trollops. The producers of *I, the Jury* pretended their screen version was "packed" with this sort of "naked fury" but, in fact, it was a pretty tame piece, causing one amused exhibitor to silently chuckle at the naïveté

Mickey Spillane's I, the Jury *became a rather tame motion picture but it was advertised as if every sexy and sadistic detail of the novel had been transferred to the screen (United Artists, 1953).*

of his somewhat disgruntled customers who "came expecting something they should have known couldn't be filmed."

The reviewer for *Boxoffice* thought Biff Elliot was "impressive and promising" as Hammer but the actor wasn't seen in a leading role again. Hoping to perpetuate the rough and tough Spillane image, the studio's publicity department did its best to make Elliot appear to be as much of a lout as the character he was portraying. The following article, which is sheer fantasy, appeared in newspapers across the country and is reprinted here both for your amusement and to give you a flavor of the period which, I'm sorry to say, wasn't all that long ago:

"Although Biff Elliot is not an adherent of that school of thought — whose principal advocate is Mickey Spillane's tough detective, Mike Hammer — which holds that the best way to discipline an erring female is by means of a well-placed bullet in the belly, he does believe that women should be treated rough. And, what's more, that they *want* to be treated that way.

Peggy Castle and Biff Elliot in a scene from **I, the Jury** *(United Artists, 1953).*

"Who is Biff Elliot?

"The mention above of Spillane and Mike Hammer is not acciden-
tal. Biff Elliot is the young television actor who was chosen by producer
Victor Saville to play the role of Hammer in 'I, the Jury,' first of the
Spillane sagas of blood and guts to be brought to the screen.

"It is Elliot's theory — stopping short, however, of Mike Hammer's
work with a gun — that the tougher and more masterful a man is, the better a woman likes it.

"'No Caspar Milquetoasts are wanted,' Elliot says. 'They're not
good promotion for men. Masculinity should be the keynote in relation-

Westerns and horror movies were the main staple of 3-D films. Pictured here is Randolph Scott from **The Stranger Wore a Gun** *(Columbia, 1953).*

ships with women. Let the girl know who's boss. He may not think so, but that's exactly what she wants, it emphasizes her own femininity.'

"In defense of his theory, Elliot points out that the violent shockers of Mickey Spillane enjoy even greater favor with women than they do with men.

"'Women readers go for Mike Hammer because they like the way he handles his girls. He'd as soon hit them as kiss them, and somehow that sort of treatment appeals to the latent atavism [sic] in women.'"

The 3-D movies continued to roll off studio assembly lines at an incredible rate, challenging directors to search for new objects to hurl at

their audiences — meteors, arrows, fists, boulders, rubber balls! Perhaps it was Frank Lovejoy's spitting at the camera that caused *Time* to wonder if Hollywood had done anything more than slap the public in the face to recapture its attention. *Film Daily* claimed the bloom was off the 3-D rose and chided the industry for its lack of character in its scramble for a quick 3-D buck. With the exception of *The Charge at Feather River*, the 3-D movies released in the summer of '53 lost money. One enterprising Detroit theater manager conducted an experiment. He simultaneously booked a flat print and a 3-D print of Columbia's *The Stranger Wore a Gun* into his duplex theater. A ticket count revealed that his patrons preferred the 3-D version so it seemed that the problem may not have been with the process but rather the quality of the movies sporting it. M-G-M decided to try an experiment of its own.

Kiss Me Kate (1953) had been a successful Broadway musical written by Samuel and Bella Spewack with songs by Cole Porter, a modernized version of Shakespeare's *The Taming of the Shrew*. Though Metro was more or less accustomed to creating their own musicals, the studio bought the rights and gave it their customary first-class treatment. It opened in six cities. In Dallas, Syracuse and Columbus it was shown in 3-D. In Houston, Rochester and Evansville it was shown flat. Reception was excellent everywhere but the 3-D engagements were even better. Dallas outgrossed the flat Houston, Rochester and Evansville by 60 percent. Rochester and Houston quickly switched to 3-D for their second week and although flat prints remained available, the studio urged exhibitors to run the stereo version.

If there was a lesson to be learned about the importance of a good story and quality production it was lost on Fred F. Sears and Columbia, who conspired to make *The Nebraskan* (1953). Sears was one of the all-time champions of unexciting potboilers, beginning his show business career as an actor, turning to directing in 1948. His list of directing credits pretty much tells the story: *Desert Vigilante, Horsemen of the Sierras* (both 1949), *Across the Badlands, Raiders of Tomahawk Creek, Lightning Guns* (all 1950), *Prairie Roundup, Ridin' the Outlaw Trail, Snake River Desperadoes, Bonanza Town, Pecos River* (all 1951), *Smokey*

(Opposite) *Ann Miller, Howard Keel, and Kathryn Grayson in a publicity still for* Kiss Me Kate, *originally slated for CinemaScope but when M-G-M couldn't get the Scope lens quickly enough the studio went with 3-D instead. It was a major hit (M-G-M, 1953).*

Canyon, The Hawk of Wild River, The Kid from Broken Gun, Last Train from Bombay, Target Hong Kong (all 1952), *Ambush at Tomahawk Gap, The 49th Man, Mission Over Korea, Sky Commando,* (all 1953), *Overland Pacific, The Miami Story, Massacre Canyon, The Outlaw Stallion* (all 1954), *Wyoming Renegades; Cell 2455, Death Row; Chicago Syndicate, Apache Ambush, Teenage Crime Wave, Inside Detroit* (all 1955), *Fury at Gunsight Pass, The Werewolf, Miami Expose, Cha-Cha-Cha Boom!, Rumble on the Docks* (all 1956), *Utah Blaine, Calypso Heat Wave, The Night the World Exploded, Escape from San Quentin* (all 1957), *The World Was His Jury, Going Steady, Crash Landing, Badman's Country, Ghost of the China Sea* (all 1958).

If you've never heard of any of these pictures there's a good reason. None of them qualifies to head the worst movies list. Such "worst" movies often achieve their own kind of greatness. Sears' output was simply dull and if he's to be remembered at all it will probably be because of his low budget rock and roll movies (*Rock Around the Clock, Don't Knock the Rock,* both 1956) or for his science fiction pictures (*Earth Vs. the Flying Saucers,* 1956 and *The Giant Claw,* 1957), and then because of other people's contributions to those films.

As if things in the 3-D market weren't bad enough, RKO produced a documentary to coincide with the sesquicentennial celebration of the purchase of the Louisiana territory from the French in 1803. *Louisiana Territory* (1953) was supposed to make you "proud of America" but it's doubtful that it did any more to boost pride than it did to build confidence in the future of 3-D movies. Many exhibitors postponed plans for 3-D conversion and with fewer theaters than initially estimated capable of playing the product, Jack Warner had to wonder.Warner wasn't ready to give up on 3-D but he felt a little discretion was in order. Warner supplied the camera and let an independent producer make *Hondo* (1953) with John Wayne as the Louis L'Amour hero.

According to a wonderful book by Hal Morgan and Dan Symmes titled *Amazing 3-D,* the camera Warners supplied had an advantage over Gunzburg's Natural Vision camera in that it could shoot closeups that were "comfortable to view." One of its disadvantages however was that one-half of the camera malfunctioned and sections of the movie were actually in 2-D but apparently not enough to damage the overall effect. It became the second highest grossing 3-D film of the decade.

But for every step forward on the 3-D quality walk there seemed to be a banana peel. In this case there were two, both tossed by Astor

Pictures. The first was *Robot Monster* (1953), made in four days for $16,000, a movie that honestly defies description, which is not to suggest that you see it. It marked the debut of actor George Nader in a starring role and contained a score by Elmer Bernstein.

Robot Monster's author, Wyott Ordung, truly one of the most unusual characters in Hollywood, explained to me how the project came about: "Phil Tucker and I had worked on a picture together and one afternoon he came to my house with his wife and told me about this picture he wanted me to write, a comedy about a guy with these big eyes. I don't write comedy and I told him so but he kept on talking about it. Actually, his wife Francine was the one who kept talking about it because Phil wasn't making a whole lot of sense. She said he wanted to make a movie about the last four people on earth after the bomb which didn't sound very funny to me. A couple of days later we shot some 3-D tests, Phil, me, and a cameraman named Gordon Abel. I wore a fire suit and had a fish bowl on my head with TV rabbit ears. Phil kept blowing his whistle which was the signal for action and I stumbled around this vacant lot in East Los Angeles shoving my hand at the camera. We used two Arriflex cameras and a mirror box. Phil thought we had better 3-D than Warner Brothers but I never saw the footage. I wrote the script and didn't hear another word until I saw Phil walking down the street in Hollywood and I asked him about it. 'You're lucky you weren't there,' he told me and I asked if there'd been any changes in my script. 'No,' he said. 'It's just the way you wrote it.' I found out later that Al Zimbalist, who produced the picture, gave my script to one of his relatives to rewrite. The guy owed him $500 and Zimbalist told him he'd forget about it if he'd rewrite the script. I couldn't believe it when I saw the thing. And I didn't make a dime."

The director told Harry Medved and Randy Dreyfuss in their *50 Worst Films of All Time* book how he managed to produce the title character on such a modest budget: "I talked to several people that I knew who had robot suits, but it was just out-of-the-way, money wise. I thought, 'Okay, I know George Barrows.' George's occupation was gorilla suit man. When they needed a gorilla in a picture they called George, because he owned his own suit and got like forty bucks a day. I thought, 'I know George will work for me for nothing. I'll get a diving helmet, put it on him, and it'll work!'"

Tucker had a row with Zimbalist and wasn't allowed to see the final cut. To see it he had to buy a ticket like everyone else. It prompted him

(Top) *Three of the Hollywood Party Girls that became* Cat-Women of the Moon. (Bottom) *Claudia Barrett and George Nader battle George Barrows as the* Robot Monster *(Astor, 1953).*

to write an open letter of apology to the *Los Angeles Times* which said in its review of the picture that it would bore even small children.

Troubled by the fact that there wasn't anything resembling a robot in the movie, or simply confused by the monster's origin, Zimbalist later changed the title to *Monster from Mars* and later *Monster from the Moon*—but a rose by any other name . . .

Astor's second 3-D sci-fi entry was *Cat-Women of the Moon* (1954) starring Sonny Tufts, once a leading man at Paramount during the 1940s when the war left a shortage of actors. After the war ended Tufts quickly found himself in potboilers like this one and he had, by the time *Cat-Women* premiered, become a camp figure. In that capacity it was a perfect vehicle for him; a comic book piece of nonsense that *The Hollywood Reporter* (apparently in a humorous frame of mind) called "well made." Again Al Zimbalist was in charge of the production and once again he managed to make a monumental stinker. And then had the incredible nerve to launch a million dollar lawsuit against one of the writers of the "My Little Margie" radio show for supposedly stealing his plot. Apparently one of the writers from the program visited the set one afternoon. Zimbalist claimed he not only stole the story but "disparaged, ridiculed, parodied, mimicked and libeled" his film by referring to it as *Cat-Women from Outer Space.*

After the Astor disasters there was nowhere for 3-D to go but up, even in the hands of Columbia who managed to round out the first decade of 3-D with one good "depthie" and one stinker.

The good news was *Miss Sadie Thompson* (1954), a musical version of Somerset Maugham's "Rain" which had been a film with Joan Crawford several decades before and a play. Columbia abandoned the Natural Vision equipment they'd previously used in favor of their own system which, like Universal's, employed the use of two cameras side by side, one upside down to put the lenses closer together. The star of the film was Rita Hayworth who was working on her fourth marriage at the time, hoping to make a comeback in films. She'd been a favorite of Harry Cohn but her romantic escapade with a married playboy in 1948 not only made her unavailable for work but caused such a scandal that by the time she returned to Hollywood a few years later she'd killed her career.

"Designed for adult consumption," said *Boxoffice* of the film. "Rita Hayworth is persuasive and provocative as the flamboyant title-roler. . . . "

A little too provocative for one 88-year-old censor who thought it was the dirtiest movie he'd ever seen. "It's rotten, lewd, immoral, just a plain raw, dirty picture, that's all," grumbled Lloyd Binford, Censor Board Chairman. He thought it should be banned even if they did snip the "filthy dance scene."

Perhaps Mr. Binford would have found some comfort in Columbia's other 3-D offering: *Drums of Tahiti* (1954), another snoozer from Bill Castle. "Possibly the triple appeal of Technicolor, 3-D and a pair of reasonably popular stars . . . may attract some business to the initial runs of this entirely unbelievable, snail-paced drama," wrote the *Boxoffice* reviewer who wondered if the picture was an act of deliberate sabotage. Even the 3-D seemed more annoying than engrossing.

After one year it began to look as if 3-D was dead. At least Robert Lippert, both a film distributor and exhibitor, thought so. According to Ed Sullivan, host of television's "Toast of the Town," New Yorkers were boycotting 3-D because of the smelly glasses. *Top Banana* and *Dial M for Murder* (1954), both intended for 3-D viewing, were shipped to theaters in flat versions. An article in one of the trade magazines boldly proclaimed that 3-D movies were not dead but it came from one of the world's largest manufacturers of 3-D equipment. What 3-D needed was a box office hit and Universal-International was about to give it one.

The success of *It Came from Outer Space* prompted U-I's front office to instigate another 3-D sci fi thriller. Understandably, the producer and director of *Outer Space*, William Alland and Jack Arnold, were assigned to the project, as well as the star, Richard Carlson. "They wanted me just because I was in something that was a hit," the actor remarked. "You make *Planet of the Apes* [1968] and you want the same cast next time. It doesn't mean *you're* a big shot."

Supposedly Alland wanted to do a movie based on a South American legend about the existence of a creature from the Devonian age still alive in the Amazon somewhere. He told the studio's resident make-up artist, Bud Westmore, to create a monster that was part human, part fish, part alligator, and part turtle that could walk on land and swim underwater. Most important of all, it couldn't look like a man in a rubber suit. Director Arnold pointed Westmore in the right direction by adding gills and fins to a sketch of the Oscar statuette.

"We gave him two arms with crab claws," said Westmore, "and we first had him with a tail and a built-in engine to operate it, so he could swish a man off his feet. But that interfered with his swimming, so we

The Creature from the Black Lagoon *temporarily pumped new life into the sagging 3-D market (Universal-International, 1954).*

cut it out. His chin, obviously, we took from the frog. His mouth? Look at any fish. The pulsating gills covered up the actor's ears—always a problem—and supplied a menacing type of movement. The head was finally shaped up on an old bust of Ann Sheridan—the only one we had with a neck.

"Monster-making," Westmore explained, "is easy after twenty-one years. You just read a lot of books on life in the lower depths of the ocean, a couple of dozen books on zoology, and an assortment of medical treatises on human anatomy; you become an expert on insect life, read up on psychology, study every picture of prehistoric monsters you can lay your hands on; you use a little common sense—and then let your

The Gill-Man and his love, Julia Adams (from Universal-International's **Creature from the Black Lagoon, *1954*).**

imagination run riot ... in a controlled sort of way, of course" ("Monsters Made to Order," by Joseph Laitin, *Collier's* 134, 12, pp. 52-53).

Easier still is to hand the assignment to your underlings which is what Westmore did. Millicent Patrick was the young lady who designed the costume for Alland's film with a little help from Jack Kevan. The result was the Gill-Man, the most popular monster of the 1950s, the real star of *The Creature from the Black Lagoon* (1954). And once Alland had his star, Harry Essex was assigned to write a script around it.

"I didn't want to do anything with a title like *Creature from the Black Lagoon*," Essex growled. "It was an embarrassment to me! But they pleaded with me to do the picture, and so I began to redevelop the whole damn thing.

"It's pretty much formula for the kind of horror stories we used to do in those days, except in this particular case I added the Beauty and the Beast theme. The whole idea was to give the Creature a kind of humanity: All he wants is to love this girl, but everybody's chasing him! It's an old formula of mine that I've used with great success" ("The Creator from the Black Lagoon," by Tom Weaver, *Fangoria*, 7, 68, p. 16).

Essex shares screenplay credit with another U-I staff writer, Arthur Ross, but the film's most memorable sequence, according to Bill Warren's magnificent chronicle of '50s sf movies *Keep Watching the Skies!*, is the product of director Arnold—the Gill-Man's underwater flirtation with leading lady Julia Adams.

"Those scenes with Ms. Adams swimming on the surface and the Creature looking up at her from below, played upon a basic fear people have about what might be lurking below the surface of any body of water," Arnold remarked. "You know the feeling, when you are swimming and something brushes your legs. It scares the hell out of you. That's the key ... the fear of the unknown. In this film I decided to exploit that fear of the unknown as much as we could. I also wanted to create sympathy for the Creature, or my little beastie as we called it, 'cause I liked him" ("The Creature Talks Among Us," by Sharon Williams and Al Taylor, *Filmfax*, 1, 4, p. 46).

Originally Glenn Strange, who'd played the Frankenstein monster in *House of Frankenstein* (1944), *House of Dracula* (1945), *and Abbott and Costello Meet Frankenstein* (1948) was considered for the role of the "beastie" but he wasn't much of a swimmer and ultimately the job went to an Olympic swimmer named Ricou Browning who likened the experience to swimming in an overcoat.

"If this combination of science-fiction drama and horror play were appraised purely for its literary, thespian and directorial values, it could be shot as full of holes as was the creature himself when he was dispatched during the film's climactic morsel of hokum," wrote the reviewer for *Boxoffice*. "But memory of what the same company garnered in revenues from its time-honored 'Frankenstein' features precludes the possibility of dismissing as readily the financial potential of the current offering. It is entirely likely that the picture, if treated to the sensational exploitation its content invites, can be a substantial grosser through an appeal to the rabid devotees of the tingling spine."

The Gill Man was back in a 3-D sequel but most theaters ran it in 2-D.

Sure enough, the Gill-Man became U-I's top grosser and earned itself a place on the sequel shelf right alongside Ma and Pa Kettle and Francis the talking mule. *Revenge of the Creature* (1955) continued the adventures of the Gill-Man who miraculously survived the barrage of bullets at the end of the first flick only to be whisked out of his Black Lagoon and dumped into a tank full of fish at Marineland in Florida. Ricou Browning was back in the rubber suit. Jack Arnold directed.

"The story had him captured and put into a tank," recalled Arnold. "I asked if they'd do us a favor and put in a net and divide the dangerous fish and put them on one side, and leave the fish that *looked* bad but were harmless on the other. They said they would. Well, when I got there the day we were ready to shoot, I went up to look at the tank and there was no net. I said, 'Fellas, I gotta get actors in there.' They said not to worry, that they feed the fish every hour on the hour and that the divers go down all of the time. I said that it was a diver's job, but these were actors — to get them to walk up a three-foot hill was a stunt. They said they couldn't use a net. Well, Ricou Browning put on the suit and dove right in. He didn't care. I looked at the cameraman and he looked at me and said, 'If you want to get those actors in there, you'd better go in yourself.' I said, 'What the hell do you mean I'd better?' So I put on the mask and jumped in, but I kept my eyes closed. Then I slowly opened one eye and I was looking down the gaping mouth of a shark. I wondered what do you do? Do you move or not move? And he just went by me (it felt like sandpaper as he rubbed against me) and I shot up out of the water and said, 'There's nothing to it, kids.' The biggest trouble that we had was with a turtle who kept biting chunks out of the monster suit" (from Author's personal interview with Jack Arnold).

Revenge of the Creature was the first film to utilize a single-strip 3-D projection system, eliminating the synchronization problem theaters had with the dual system as well as the need for a intermission.

Early on, when *Bwana Devil* was still packing them in and DeMille was still trying to decide whether to shoot his epic about Moses in 3-D or CinemaScope, a couple of guardians of public morality began to wonder if the added realism of 3-D might call for an overhaul of the Production Code. Violence that might have been acceptable in a conventional film might be too strong in 3-D. And what about the possible prurient effects of seeing some shapely lady like Marilyn Monroe in 3-D? Howard Hughes wanted to find out.

In 1941, Hughes caused a tremendous stink by releasing *The Outlaw* without the Motion Picture Association of America's approval. The MPAA was anticipating trouble with the fictionalized and sexy account of Billy the Kid long before they actually saw it, due mostly to Hughes' widely publicized breast quest which ended with actress Jane Russell — once introduced by Bob Hope as "the two and only Miss Russell" — for whom Hughes had designed a specially engineered bra to accent her 38-inch chest. And her chest was what the movie was really about. So when the MPAA demanded cuts and changes, Hughes ignored them. He sat on the movie for a few years then sent it out without the seal and was thrown out of the MPAA for doing it. In retaliation, Hughes

Jane Russell (center) *in 3-D! She'll knock* both *your eyes out, claimed the ads. Seen here with Mary McCarty* (left) *and Joyce MacKenzie. (From* **The French Line,** *RKO, 1954).*

filed an antitrust suit and applied for an injunction to force the MPAA to give his picture their seal. The judge thought the whole thing was simply a publicity stunt and refused to take action. The suit was dropped when the MPAA pointed out that it hadn't the power to prevent theaters from showing the picture and all that Hughes had succeeded in doing was to provoke the association into implementing stricter rules and fines.

Ten years later Hughes was at it again. The ads he approved for *The French Line* (1954) proudly displayed Jane Russell in a revealing costume with large cut-outs. The copy read: "J.R. in 3-D . . . need we say more?" Of course Hughes did say more, in case some potentially interested customer didn't get the point. He promised that the film would knock *both* your eyes out! Again the MPAA refused to give the picture a seal and again Hughes proceeded without one.

The picture had been booked by the Fanchon and Marco theater circuit as part of a contract and F&M's Fox Theater in St. Louis was chosen for the world premiere. The city's police station was flooded with calls from outraged citizens. With the approval of the Archbishop, the Council of Catholic Men sent a letter of protest that was read aloud in the city's Catholic churches. The chief of police promised to look into the matter and sent a few of his men to the theater with orders to stop the performance and make some arrests if things got too hot. But the screening continued as planned with nary an empty seat in the house.

All of the commotion had unintentionally stirred up interest in the picture. It was the biggest opening day the theater had seen in six years. The manager, Edward Arthur, told the press that until the cops showed up he'd been unaware that there was any problem. And while everyone waited to see if the MPAA would slap Hughes with the $25,000 fine they'd threatened him with, producer Samuel Goldwyn fired off a letter to MPAA president Eric Johnston, strongly urging him to avoid similar situations in the future by amending the code.

"Audiences today realize what creative people have always known," Goldwyn wrote: "that drama is worthless unless it has integrity and resembles life. To portray life honestly on the screen requires a greater degree of latitude, within the bounds of decency, than exists under the code."

As the MPAA war raged on, *The French Line* continued to be, as *Boxoffice* predicted, "a money attraction." Controversy aside, it was just another miserable movie that did nothing to further the 3-D cause. When *The Film Daily* asked, "If 3D is dead, who killed it?" the answer was too obvious. One had only to look at the films being offered in 1954:

Taza, Son of Cochise with Rock Hudson in the title role.

Money from Home with Dean Martin and Jerry Lewis chased by gangsters.

Phantom of the Rue Morgue with Karl Malden chewing scenery in yet another version of Poe's story "Murders in the Rue Morgue."

The Mad Magician with Vincent Price in a pale imitation of *House of Wax.*

Southwest Passage with Rod Cameron battling injuns.

With the writing clearly on the wall Gig Young, just beginning his career in acting, wondered if it was advisable to accept the lead role in *Gog* (1954), a low budget science fiction flick from United Artists. Herb Strock, the director, told him to pass on it. "It's going to be a dud," Strock told him, "and it won't do your career one bit of good." Young thanked him and left the part for another actor.

By the end of 1954 3-D movies were gasping for breath. (Top) Vincent Price tries his sleight-of-hand with Mary Murphy in a scene from The Mad Magician, *Columbia's answer to* House of Wax. *(Bottom) Fernando Lamas, Rhonda Fleming and Brian Keith facing imminent danger of death by boredom in* Jivaro *(Paramount, 1954).*

By the summer of '55, 3-D had gone the way of the Davy Crockett coonskin caps. *Jivaro* was Paramount's final film in 3-D as was *Dangerous Mission* for RKO. It seemed almost malicious of Fox, having won the battle over 3-D with its CinemaScope process, to release *Gorilla at Large*. It was like firing a bullet into a corpse.

As for Cecil B. DeMille . . . he decided to make his Moses movie in VistaVision.

From time to time 3-D would venture forth, like a bashful suitor, only to be buried again beneath the weight of the inferior productions it attempted to enhance, eventually becoming a tool of porno movie producers, which was an improvement in some ways but hardly likely to elevate the credibility (to say nothing of the respectability) of the process. Arch Oboler took another crack at it in 1966 with *The Bubble*. Oboler had managed to make some improvements on the process since the release of his *Bwana Devil* but the movie was a bore. It began to look as if the quick buck artists had killed 3-D once and for all. Then, on Wednesday, August 19, 1970, the following comments, by Ronald Gold, appeared in *Variety:*

"Producer-director Joseph Strick, who broke new cinematic ground with 'Ulysses,' hopes to do so again—in an altogether different direction—by making a theatrical motion picture shot and projected entirely with laser light. The result, he predicts, will be an entirely new kind of three-dimensional cinema that—without glasses—would give the audiences the impression of actual objects present before them (not flattened-out screen images), some of which could appear to be resting directly on their laps.

"The process, known as holography or 'lensless photography,' has been used previously for still pictures (if you move slightly, you can see the object from another angle, or around its corners) and is currently being employed by stage designers, but until recently it was unsuited to motion pictures, since the slightest movement would destroy the image. Now, according to Strick, recent experiments with pulsating laser light make it possible to shoot objects in motion.

"At the present state of development, Strick says, he will only be able to use interiors, since sunlight is 'diffused' and laser light is 'coherent' (all the light waves go in the same direction). Nonetheless he is looking about for a suitable property (perhaps Berthold Brecht's 'Galileo') and is hoping to be in production, on a $1,000,000 budget, in about nine months."

Portions of The Mask *were in red and green 3-D. It didn't help make it exciting (Warner Bros, 1961).*

An article in *Boxoffice* magazine just a few months earlier had announced that the "father of holography," Dr. Dennis Gabor, had been awarded a patent for a new method of projecting three-dimensional movies that could be seen without glasses and that we'd be hearing (or seeing) from him shortly. The Sherpix people couldn't wait. They made a pot of money with a 3-D porno flick called *The Stewardesses* (1971), then bought the rights to *House of Wax* and reissued it the following year. Children who'd never experienced stereovision went wild, prompting Universal to re-release *It Came from Outer Space* and *The Creature from the Black Lagoon* on a double bill. Unfortunately, Universal opted for the red and green image rather than the superior Polaroid process and people who'd never seen the latter wondered what all the fuss was about since the image with red and green glasses only works during bright sequences and then not very well.

Andy Warhol's Frankenstein (1974), also known as *Flesh for Frankenstein,* became the highest grossing 3-D film ever, even with its X-rating. Or maybe because of it. *Playboy* called it the most "outrageously gruesome epic ever unleashed," with Joe Dallesandro as the doctor obsessed with creating life, making a curtain speech with his heart dangling on the end of a spear.

This second 3-D revival came to a climax with the release of *A*P*E* (1976), made on the cheap in Korea to cash in on the publicity Dino De Laurentiis had been generating with his multimillion dollar remake of *King Kong* (1976). Paramount got an injunction against the picture. In retrospect it is difficult to determine which film was worse.

At the same time a few revival theaters began unearthing prints of some of the earlier 3-D movies and for the first time audiences were able to see things like Hitchcock's *Dial M for Murder* which had never been seen in 3-D before. But the novelty burned itself out as fast as it had before because the time simply wasn't right. But in the 1980s the time was ideal. Ronald Reagan was in the White House, and the 1950s were here again. Viet Nam was forgotten and Ronnie was looking for someone to fight. The movement to secure equal rights for women was defeated, wrestling and the Three Stooges were back on television, outraged parents were attacking rock and roll music, '50s-style malt shops began popping up, and the kids began sporting ugly butch haircuts. It seemed only fitting to have another 3-D craze. It began, as did the first one, outside of the Hollywood system.

Comin' at Ya (1981) was an Italian spoof of Westerns, not very funny but loaded with into-the-camera effects. Like *Bwana Devil* it got terrible reviews and cleaned up at the box office — $13 million before it was done. That was all producer Charles Band needed to hear. By the following year he had *Parasite* (1982) in the theaters. "The research I had done on 3-D during preproduction was very negative," Band recalled. "No one wanted to hear about it; they thought it was not really

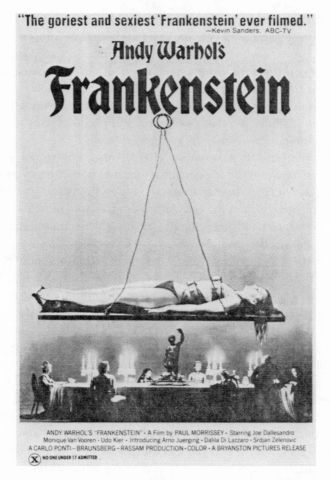

The X-rated Frankenstein *became the highest grossing 3-D film ever (Bryanston, 1974).*

a help. Some distributors I talked to pointed out all the difficulties with projection lenses and the glasses, and about how 3-D had died in the '50s and that I shouldn't fool with it." (quoted in "Parasite," by David Everitt, *The Bloody Best of Fangoria*, p. 66).

His movie was on *Variety's* list of top grossers after its first two weeks in New York.

Band, who once said that his biggest ambition was to make 2000 movies by the end of the century, stuffed as many gruesome effects into *Parasite* as his tiny budget could afford, but it was merely a primer for

Friday the 13th Part 3 (1982), a celebration of sadistic mayhem. In the third of the most successful series since Francis the mule, characters are chopped in half, poked in every possible orifice, and crushed till their eyeballs pop out. (It was hardly the sort of honesty that Sam Goldwyn had pleaded for in his letter to the MPAA.)

Friday the 13th Part 3's producers were especially proud of the scene of a woman speared through her eye:

"They did a side shot of her taking a reaction upon impact and falling back into the water," explained the makeup artist, Doug White, "and then they cut to her turning sideways with the tip of the spear coming toward the camera for the 3-D effect. But they cut out the reaction because they said it looked too good" ("Doug White and Makeup Effects Lab," by David Everitt, *The Bloody Best of Fangoria*, p. 35).

The older 3-D movies began showing up on local television stations in 3-D across the country. *The Mad Magician* was shown in Los Angeles on Channel 9's horror show hosted by Elvira whose lack of wit is only partly compensated for by her ample bosom. I confess to being involved, albeit briefly, in an ill-conceived attempt to repackage *Robot Monster* for a 3-D showing on cable TV. The sponsors of this enterprise wanted to add new color footage and dub "funny" dialog into the old footage, as if anyone could possibly top what was already there. During the development of the new script one of the producers had an idea for a gag which I feel is worth relating here to succinctly illustrate the real reason why 3-D movies wear out their welcome. We were in a recording studio, in the middle of an embarrassing song for the main titles, when this producer who shall remain nameless took me to one side and said, "I was thinking that it would really be funny if we had the robot monster knock over a garbage can in an alley." I waited for the rest of it but that's all there was.

Of course the major studios finally got involved with a pair of sequels. From Filmways came *Amityville 3-D* and from Universal *Jaws 3-D* (both 1983). The latter film was originally offered to director Joe Dante but ultimately was given to a former production designer and art director, Joe Alves. It was Alves' first shot at directing and he felt 3-D would give him an edge. Production began with Stereovision which was dropped after a week in favor of Arrivision, which Alves believed was a superior system because it had a wider variety of lenses. "The problem with *Comin' At Ya*, and a lot of these cheaper 3-D films, is that they were done with inferior optics," explained Alves, "resulting in an imperfect match of left-right images, resulting in blurring and ghosting, and headaches for the audience. On our film, the left and right images are very well matched, and the photography is very clean; it's restful to the eye, and though we have occasional effects where things do emerge toward the audience from the plane of projection, you come out of the film without a headache" ("Joe Alves and Jaws 3-D," by Brick Thornshaw, *Fangoria* 1, 29).

Things finally settled down and it looked like 3-D was headed for obscurity again until it found a home at Disneyland in a production titled *Captain E-O* featuring the dynamic Michael Jackson before he became Diana Ross. 3-D never looked better. And for a change it's being used to enhance something rather than salvage it.

And nobody's complaining about the glasses.

Five

Blubberscope, Whatever . . .

*I kept reading in the paper about all these people with
different processes, which were absolutely* nothing —
*wide screen, narrow screen, upside down screen, Blub-
berscope, whatever. . . . Dynamation came out of it.*
— **Ray Harryhausen, Special Effects Genius**

Inspired by 3-D and CinemaScope, new technical innovations
were developed at an astounding rate — hardly a difficult task since, as
often as not, these "innovations" were nothing more than a fancy name.

I remember sitting at my desk, in my bedroom, drawing as I often
did as a child, listening to music on the radio, when an announcer broke
in to plug *The 5,000 Fingers of Dr. T* (1953), "the first musical
Wonderama starring Peter Lind Hayes and Mary Healy." Although I
can't say for sure, my guess would be that the announcer was Art
Gilmore who sold people down the river regularly and with gay abandon. If you went to the movies at all during the '50s, '60s, and '70s you

were familiar with Art 'cause his was the voice on 80 percent of the coming attraction previews. During the days of the double feature, Art was
spliced in between the trailers: a brief little clip of a blue sky with
spotlights waving back and forth and Art's voice saying, "Plus this
outstanding feature on the same program." And then there'd be scenes
from something awful like *Monkeys, Go Home!* (1967).

Anyway, Art sounded pretty excited about this movie he was
huckstering but then Art was easily the most enthusiastic guy around.
The man could get worked up over the most unexceptional things. But
at six I was green. I wanted to know more about this Wonderama
business. I put my pencil down and listened.

"For 5,000 happy thrills of song, laughter, and love," Art bubbled,
"don't miss *The 5,000 Fingers of Dr. T*, the lightest, brightest Stanley
Kramer production ever!"

At the time, of course, that remark flew right past me. Thinking
back on it now, it's pretty funny. With a roster of deadly serious and
often depressing movies to his credit — *Home of the Brave* (1949), *The
Men* (1950), *Death of a Salesman* (1951) — Stanley Kramer wasn't exactly
known for his good cheer.

" . . . So big they had to use every sound stage in Columbia's studios
to hold its exciting sets, so different they had to invent new instru-
ments. . . . " On and on and on Art babbled but never did he tell me
about Wonderama. I was pretty sore about it but in fairness it wasn't
Art's fault. There was nothing more for him to say about it. Wonderama
was just another thread in the Emperor's new clothes.

Here then are some other "amazing screen miracles." Many, like
Wonderama, are duck eggs. Others, surprisingly enough, are genuine.
As you look them over don't be put off by the smell of sawdust in the air.

Amazoscope

See: Mattascope.

Aroma-Rama

A system developed by Charles Weiss whereby various odors are
pumped into auditoriums through theater ventilation systems, hope-
fully corresponding with the image on the screen. Used to enhance a

European travelogue, *Behind the Great Wall* (1959), purchased by Walter Reade, Jr., who promised that "none of our smells will be objectionable." It was an obvious attempt to take advantage of the publicity surrounding another more sophisticated odor process, Smell-O-Vision.

Cinemagic

An attempt to blend live action with line drawings, this process was the creation of Norman Maurer, a comic book artist. The son-in-law of Moe Howard of the Three Stooges, Maurer was still in the development stage of what he then called Artiscope when producer Sidney Pink, once Arch Oboler's partner during the *Bwana Devil* days, decided to use it in a feature film. With Maurer's invention, Pink hoped to make an incredible outer space epic for peanuts by simply drawing most of the sets. Performers wore white makeup and were photographed in black and white. The dark areas of the negative were removed with acid and supposedly went through four separate printings with Maurer's Artiscope lens. The result, printed in red, was a burned out effect more easily achieved through solarization.

The name was changed from Artiscope to Cinemagic which made its debut in Pink's *The Angry Red Planet* (1959), originally distributed by Sino Productions, ultimately bought by American International who saw gold in all that red. AIP sent the following message to its string of exhibitors: "Cinemagic, acclaimed by leading showmen as the most amazing new motion picture process since the invention of the camera, will take audiences into the world of the fourth dimension. We feel that *The Angry Red Planet* in Cinemagic and the new Eastman 5250 color [nothing more than a new stock number] must be the most talked about science fiction picture of the year." According to AIP's publicity department, Cinemagic had the power to increase depth perception a thousandfold. *Variety* conceded that it may have taken "considerable ingenuity" to produce the effect but after all was said and done it simply wasn't worth it. *The Los Angeles Times* thought "the potentially clever blurring process" was sabotaged by "producer Pink's use of cheap, clearly unreal backdrops." Less kind critics said a red lollipop wrapper in front of the projector would have worked just as well. Cinemagic was used one more time, with better success, in *The Three Stooges in Orbit* (1962). But it was never, in its top form, anything to write home about.

Cinemagic promised the impossible. (American International, 1959).

Duo-Vision

The technique of splitting the screen image so that several bits of business were on screen simultaneously is an idea as old as movies themselves. It's been used several times to show both ends of a telephone conversation in one scene, as in Universal-International's

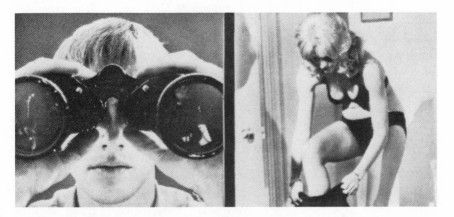

Randolph Roberts watches Diane McBain in this demonstration of Duo-Vision (from M-G-M's Wicked Wicked, *1973).*

Pillow Talk (1959). Filmmakers began experimenting with the technique in the mid–1960s and for a brief time it became trendy. Director John Frankenheimer had ten or twelve images on the screen at a given moment in *Grand Prix* (1966) to show the various actions of his race cars and their drivers. A similar effect was seen during a robbery sequence in *The Thomas Crown Affair* (1968). As late as 1976 director Brian De Palma employed the device for his thriller *Carrie,* much to the detriment of the sequence in which it was used.

With the possible exception of *Woodstock* (1970), the effect has generally proved more distracting than exciting. But in 1973 writer-producer-director Richard L. Bare made an entire movie of double images, *Wicked, Wicked,* a suspense drama about a psycho-killer at an old seaside resort. Bare began his career as a director at Warner Bros. with films like *Smart Girls Don't Talk* (1948), and *Flaxy Martin,* crime dramas all. He supposedly cooked up this Duo-Vision idea because it lent itself "to showing truth and untruth, flashbacks in time, visions of the future or cause and effect without abrupt interruption of the story's main continuity." Neither the concept nor Mr. Bare has been seen since.

Dynamation

Trademark name coined by special effects technician Ray Harryhausen to describe his combination of stop-motion puppet animation, rear screen projection, and blue screen matte work, derived from "dynamic" and "animation." For over 20 years Harryhausen, though the master of visual wizardry, was ignored by the Academy of Motion Picture Arts and Sciences because his work was featured in low budget programmers in the beginning and later in films made outside the studio system in Spain or England.

At age 13 Harryhausen's fancy was captured by the classic *King Kong* (1933). He began to experiment with three dimensional animation, accomplished like cartoon animation a frame at a time. He worked on the now famous George Pal Puppetoons and finally got the opportunity to work for his idol Willis O'Brien, the man responsible for the effects work in *Kong.* Harryhausen was O'Brien's right hand man on *Mighty Joe Young* (1949) which earned O'Brien an Academy Award though Harryhausen did most of the animation. Some years later Harryhausen teamed with producer Charles Schneer, an association that lasted 30 years.

It was critical to streamline O'Brien's methods of blending stop-motion puppets with live action, which is precisely what Harryhausen did. He eliminated the need for glass paintings and miniature sets by making more extensive use of split screen and rear projection screens. The result was less fanciful but more realistic (and less costly). After three movies with Producer Schneer this technique was introduced to the public as Dynamation in *The 7th Voyage of Sinbad* (1958). His previous films had been photographed in black and white and the addition of color for *Sinbad* presented a problem when the proper film stock was available for Harryhausen's rear projection plates.

"And the minute you duped it by projection, your colors deteriorated and it got grainy," Harryhausen lamented. "In those days, I had to flash the film with light in a laboratory to reduce contrast on the raw stock before plate photography. Then, I had to come up with a rear projection system in which the grain of the screen was reduced with a vibrating source. Sometimes the problems are unavoidable" (quoted in "Careers," by Paul Mandell, *Cinemagic*, vol. 8, no. 1, p. 57). Grainy or not the effects sequences were tremendous and the film was highly successful. Dynamation became SuperDynamation for the next Harryhausen-Schneer collaboration, *The 3 Worlds of Gulliver* (1960). And over the years it's been labelled a number of different ways but the process is always the same. "It is always a frame-by-frame process which

(Top) *Special effects master Ray Harryhausen with two of his creations.* (Bottom) *The incredible skeleton fight from* The 7th Voyage of Sinbad, *the first film in Dynamation. That's Kathryn Grant watching Kerwin Mathews being backed into a corner (Columbia, 1958).*

takes time," said Harryhausen. "One of the greatest problems in this
field is that after everyone's forgotten the picture you have to go on
keeping excited and interested in what you are doing in order to go on
for another year. Sometimes it gets a bit dismal but I survive" (quoted
in "Clash of the Titans," by Robert Greenberger, *Fangoria*, vol. 2, no.
12, p. 56).

Clash of the Titans (1981) was Harryhausen's most expensive effort
and one of M-G-M's top grossers of the year but Schneer has been
unable to secure backing for a similar project and it appears that it will
be Harryhausen's final film. At 67 he's decided to turn his talents to
sculpting. "I'm trying to assemble a museum of my work, which will be
perpetuated after I'm gone," he says. "Also, Diana [his wife] and I have
a house in Spain and we love going there to be in the sunshine. Diana
is learning to paint. We have a good time in Spain. I manage to keep
busy. I never seem to be bored" (quoted in "Farewell to Fantasy Films,"
by Steve Swires, *Starlog*, vol. 11, no. 127, p. 64).

Dynarama

See: Dynamation. Dynarama was the name Columbia's publicity
department put on their advertisements for *Sinbad and the Eye of the
Tiger* (1977) and a re-release of *The Seventh Voyage of Sinbad*.

Electrolitic Dynamation

See: Dynamation. Electrolitic Dynamation was something coined
by the publicity department for the release of *20,000,000 Miles to Earth*
(1957) although it did not appear on any of the advertisements.

Emergo

Brainchild of producer-director William Castle, advertised as if it
were some sort of 3-D without glasses — "The thrills fly right into the audience!" All that flew was a luminous skeleton on a fishing line during
a key moment in *House on Haunted Hill*.

Another victim of The Crater Lake Monster, *brought to life by Fantamation and the talents of David Allen (Crown International, 1977).*

Fantamation

Has the same ingredients as Dynamation used to bring to life *The Crater Lake Monster* (1977). The talented David Allen, assisted by Randy Cook and Phil Tippet, was in charge of the stop motion special effects.

Like Ray Harryhausen, Allen was inspired at an early age by *King Kong*. Harryhausen's *7th Voyage of Sinbad* also had a great influence on him. After a few experiments in stop-frame photography he became involved in an amateur film called *Equinox* (1969) and for a number of years was a regular at Cascade Pictures where he worked on numerous commercials including the "Poppin Fresh Doughboy" and "Mrs. Butterworth."

During that period Allen took a leave of absence to work in England on the film *When Dinosaurs Ruled the Earth* (1970). His work has been the saving grace in films like *Q* (1982) and *Ghoulies II* (1987). Allen has become the patron saint of short-sighted filmmakers who are rarely, if ever, a match for his skills.

Fantascope

Described by producer Edward Small as the "combining of animate and inanimate: real people with stop-action puppets and other special effects. When a movie-goer hears the word animation he immediately thinks of drawings and cartoons . . . but Fantascope goes a step further and delivers the dimension of depth. At long last, film process shots are treated in color as well."

Fantascope was a variation on Dynamation, just as the film in which it was used, *Jack the Giant Killer* (1962), was a variation of Ray Harryhausen's *The 7th Voyage of Sinbad.* Legend has it that Harryhausen had come to Small's office in the early 1950s with sketches for a proposed Sinbad movie but he couldn't get past Small's secretary. Years later, when Harryhausen's Sinbad movie made a pot of money for Columbia, Small hoped to trade on that success by essentially making the same film, using the same actors and the same director. So intent was Small to duplicate the previous picture he not only insisted that many of the puppets resemble the puppets from Sinbad but move like them as well, down to a frame count. Small's movie lost money and thereafter he supposedly went into a tizzy at the very mention of stop-motion photography.

HypnoMagic

Gimmick name coined by producer Charles Bloch to promote his film *The Hypnotic Eye* (1959). Toward the end of the movie, Jacques Bergerac (in the role of The Great Desmond, a stage hypnotist) conducts a demonstration of hypnotism. He asks that the house lights be turned on, which is the cue for the projectionist to raise the lights about 40 percent. At this point the audience in the movie and the audience in the theater merge as Bergerac speaks directly into the camera. Gil Boyne, the director of the American Hypnological Society (if there is such a thing), was hired to coach Bergerac for this stunning moment in screen history, probably more as a publicity stunt than an attempt to add authenticity to the proceedings. According to the following press release, Bergerac actually hypnotized his costar Merry Anders:

"The shapely blonde actress agreed to let her costar put her into an actual hypnotic trance for the scene — if he could.

Order "HypnoMagic" Balloons From Your Allied Artists Exchange

SPOT THESE SIGNS
NEAR DOORMAN

Your local Allied Artists branch is handling the HypnoMagic balloons. Order them when you book the picture. The cost is $20 per thousand. Please allow plenty of time for shipment. Special express or air shipments will cost extra as the balloons are being sold at cost!

The balloons come with "air retainer" mouth-

piece which enables them to be easily inflated and closed-off. They are imprinted with the catch-line:—"You can't resist 'The Hypnotic Eye'," and an illustration of the eye.

The nominal cost of the balloons will be reflected many times over at the box office. Sell Hypno-Magic big and it will pay off big for you!

IMPORTANT!
KEEP "THE HYPNOTIC EYE" BALLOON . . . IT IS PART OF THE PICTURE!

DO NOT INFLATE IT UNTIL YOU ARE INSTRUCTED TO DO SO FROM THE SCREEN!

An audience caught in the grip of "HypnoMagic," in this moment from The Hypnotic Eye *(Allied Artists, 1959).*

"Newspaper men were on the set as witnesses, and after the scene had been filmed they questioned Merry closely. Had she really been hypnotized or only acting? Could she remember anything that had happened?

"'Of course I remember,' she said. 'Hypnosis is a state of altered consciousness, but not of unconsciousness. I remember everything Jacques said and everything I did at his command. But at the time it seemed, I had to obey and was perfectly capable of doing whatever he told me.'

"He told her, for one thing, that her body had become as rigid as stone. Then he lifted her bodily and stretched her between two chairs, her neck resting on the back of one, her ankles on the back of the other.

"'If I hadn't been hypnotized I'd never have been able to stay there,' she pointed out. 'But of course Jacques and I have been practicing this hypnotism business for days and we knew from past performance that he could put me under. Otherwise,' she told the reporters, laughing, 'you'd never have been invited today.'"

Even if Bergerac was capable of hypnotizing an audience he would have been prohibited from doing so by law.

"They don't, of course, experience the actual sensations, but the psychological effects of them," explained producer Block. "By inserting this scene just before the climax, we are able to give people the illusion of being catapulted into the climax itself.

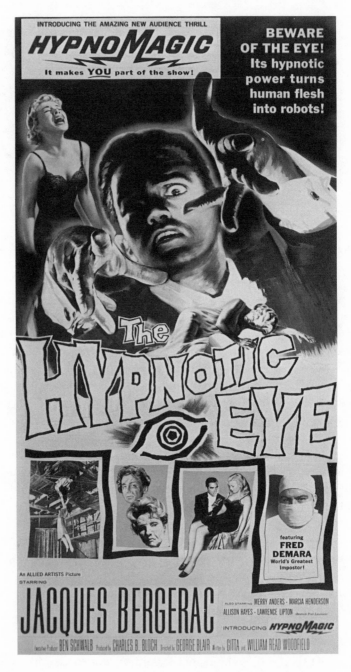

Ad art for HypnoMagic *and* The Hypnotic Eye.

"And the potentialities of this new technique are tremendous. Hyp-noMagic opens up whole new vistas to the director and is bound to work an organic change throughout the medium—something like when pictures first learned to talk. Now they're discovering the value of psychological research to dramatic art, with new ways of communicating, new ways of reaching people where they live."

A scream at the beginning of reel 9 was the projectionist's cue to turn off the lights.

HypnoVista

James Nicholson, president of American International Pictures, spliced a 13 minute lecture on hypnotism by Dr. Emile Franchel to the beginning of *Horrors of the Black Museum* (1959).

"The doc gets the jump on his audiences—at least the younger ones—right off by telling them that only idiots and fools can't be hypnotized," wrote Jack Moffit in *The Hollywood Reporter*. "Thereafter at the previews, the kids hastened to prove their mental health by yawning when the doc told them to, forcing their hands apart at his bidding, shivering when he suggested a blue light was cold, and mopping their brows when he said a red light was blistering. Such handy exercises to convince yourself you are not an idiot are certainly worth the price of admission and while all this is but remotely related to the story that follows, it does supply a sort of exploitation gimmick an exhibitor can use to promote word-of-mouth interest in his offering."

According to AIP's publicity department, Dr. Franchel was an internationally renowned psychologist from Sussex, England: "At an early age it was discovered that he had powers bordering on the occult. Over the years, he has had many honors and degrees bestowed upon him and is recognized as an outstanding practitioner in his field. He has worked closely with many leading psychiatrists, particularly during World War II in aiding battle worn service men. After many years of operating his own school in London, he migrated to the United States in 1951. He spent 3½ years in New York studying the outstanding American psychology techniques. In 1955 Emile started on a lecture tour which carried him through 14 states in as many weeks. He eventually arrived in California and settled in Hollywood where in February of 1956, he appeared on a locally produced television show and conducted 'live'

HypnoVista promised an incredible motion picture experience. A promise that was broken (American International, 1959).

experiments in the controversial field of pre-birth age regression. The show received the highest rating ever accorded a television program. From this came his own television show exploring the human mind. He conducts a non-profit 'Hypno-Mercy' foundation working with terminal cases of painful diseases. He has also made bold ventures into the field of 'hypno-criminology.'"

And in 1959, Emile was sticking hypodermic needles into a woman's arm to help peddle a sadistic horror film to young children.

Illusion-O

At the beginning of *13 Ghosts* (1960), producer-director William Castle appeared to explain how to use the "Ghost Viewers" the audience had been given upon entering the theater. There were two strips of cellophane on the viewer, one red the other blue. The red strip made the ghosts appear. The blue strip erased them. The words "use viewer" flashed at the bottom of the screen shortly before each ghostly sequence. Not content with having made a fool of everyone once, Castle returned at the end of the story to suggest using the viewer at home.

"He knew every gimmick in a horror movie," said writer Robb White of Castle. "We used the same ol' dead head in every movie, practically, because we owned it. We bought it for $12.50. That was the head that was in *Psycho*. They rented it from us. And then we had an old warty hand. He had to have that hand in every movie. He had the squeaking door hinges. He had the girl in the white nightgown. He had every horror movie gimmick that he could put together" (quoted in "Scripting the Castles of Horror," by John Wooley, *Fangoria*, vol. 3, no. 43, p. 14).

Magnascope

Introduced by Paramount Pictures with the release of *Chang* (1927). During certain moments the projectionist would switch lenses to increase the size of the image. It proved to be rather distracting to say nothing of the worry it caused the exhibitors who were afraid they'd be forced to build larger theaters to accommodate larger screens. The idea was dropped and Paramount head Adolph Zukor assured everyone there'd be no more messing with the screen size until things got a lot better in the motion picture industry. Or a lot worse.

Mattascope

Uninspired term, no doubt coined by Columbia's publicity department, to describe the blue screen and split screen shots in *The 30 Foot Bride of Candy Rock* (1959). Apparently the publicity department couldn't make up its mind for in the preview trailer for the film these unexceptional special effects fell under the umbrella term "Amazoscope."

Mystimation

A truly unusual combination of stop motion animation, cartooning, split screen, mattes, rear screen and other special effects to simulate the look of the woodcuts that accompanied the text of many of Jules Verne's first editions. It was employed by Karel Zeman for *The Fabulous World of Jules Verne* (1958). Born in Moravia, Czechoslovakia, Zeman had been a window dresser and a poster artist before entering the film business. His films — *Christmas Dream* (1946), *Prokouk the Bureaucrat* (1947), *Inspiration* (1949), *King Lavra* (1950), *The Treasure of Bird Island* (1952), *Journey to the Beginning of Time* (1955), *Baron Munchausen* (1962), *The Jester's Tale* (1964), *The Stolen Airship* (1966), *Mr. Sverdac's Ark* (1968) — always displayed a unique vision and wild experimentation.

Percepto

Advertised as "an astounding new dimension in feeling and fright," it was another gimmick by William Castle that supposedly made the audience part of the action on the screen. The ads for *The Tingler* (1959) read: "Actual shock-sensations and physical reactions experienced by the actors will be felt by you—in all their terrifying impact!" Writer Robb White recalled how it all came about: ". . . Bill came into the studio and said, 'Hey, write me a story about shaking the seats.' He said, 'We'll put little motors under the seats and at certain points we'll have 'em shake, you know, have the seats shake.' So we did that. And the kids came with screwdrivers and stole all the motors" (quoted in "Scripting the Castles of Horror," by John Wooley, *Fangoria*, vol. 3, no. 43, p. 12).

Perceptovision

Touted as "the newest marvel of the motion picture world!" by United Artists' publicity department, it was a meaningless term for some old-fashioned split screen and blue screen work by producer-director Bert I. Gordon. Gordon had dabbled in special effects for

(Opposite) *Lou Costello and Dorothy Provine in* **The 30 Foot Bride of Candy Rock,** *filmed in Mattascope. Or Amazoscope. Or something (Columbia, 1959).*

Two scenes from Karel Zeman's remarkable The Fabulous World of Jules Verne, *filmed in Mystimation (Warner Bros., 1961).*

Cathy O'Donnell is pictured here in this demonstration footage from Terror in the Haunted House *(1959), showing "PsychoRama" in action.*

almost a decade before this picture, yet after seven movies he still hadn't gotten the hang of it. He was like the magician who couldn't palm his cards quick enough. Any child growing up in the 1950s who was interested in learning how special effects were created is indebted to Bert Gordon. You didn't exactly learn how effects were done by watching one of Gordon's films but the work was so clumsy it did offer a clue.

PsychoRama

Made its first appearance in the motion picture *My World Dies Screaming* which was later retitled *Terror in the Haunted House* (1959). A demonstration of PsychoRama was held for the press at the Beverly Canon theater in Hollywood, California, and Hazel Flynn of the *Hollywood Citizen News* had this to say about it: "The reel shown offered a dramatic sequence from what probably would have ordinarily been a regular mystery thriller. There is no question however, that by projecting the words death death death multitudinous times without the audience realizing it and blood blood blood in like fashion the reel was heightened in its dramatic effect."

These images, on screen just long enough to register in the subconscious, caused Ms. Flynn to question the producer's right to mess with the minds of the public, and the National Association of Broadcasters agreed. At the time of this film's release, the use of subliminal images was under attack, especially in advertising. (One Iowa theater owner used it to stimulate interest in his snack bar and had his best month ever.)

Terror in the Haunted House and *A Date with Death*, released the same year, both attempted to exploit the controversy surrounding this subject. The NAB and the Federal Communications Commission eventually outlawed subliminal advertising.

Regiscope

Yet another fanciful name for stop-motion puppetry combined with live action, this time for the science fiction western *The Beast of Hollow Mountain* (1956), produced by Edward and William Nassour. Usually a single puppet is moved into different positions for each frame of film but in this film, for all of the far shots of the animal, replacement puppets were used. That is to say there was a different puppet for each frame of film. This technique allows the same latitude afforded a cartoon animator such as the ability to stretch and squeeze an arm or leg, the sort of detail that makes a thing seem lifelike. Edward Nassour had another explanation for Regiscope, reported in an article that appeared in *The New York Times:* "The Regiscope machine predetermines every movement of any inanimate objects to be used in the motion picture

Red Morgan (left) and Lew Marman check to see if Stephanie Farnay is wearing a bra, in this scene from the PsychoRama chiller **A Date with Death** *(Pacific International, 1959).*

and records it on a tape. The 'actor' is then electronically controlled in all of its motion. To insure complete fidelity of movement, the Regiscope operator can rehearse the 'actor' in its motions in front of him before filming begins. The director can select the best of the 'performances' in the rehearsals and, from that moment, there is no deviation because of the electronic controls."

As far as I know, *The Beast of Hollow Mountain* was the first stop-motion movie in CinemaScope.

Sensurround

An addition to the soundtrack that when decoded caused a mild vibration, developed by Universal for their disaster epic *Earthquake* (1974), and subsequently used in *Midway* (1976), *Rollercoaster* (1977), and the theatrical release of some episodes of the television series *Battlestar: Galactica* (1979).

A special amplifier and 10 to 20 speakers were required to produce the desired effect and most theaters couldn't handle the stress. One theater in Hollywood had to install a net just below the ceiling to catch falling plaster. When *Earthquake* was shown on a local Los Angeles television station it was simulcast on FM radio, supposedly to give the viewer at home the same experience that people had when they saw the movie in the theater. It's my understanding that the pitch of the vibrating frequency is out of radio transmission range but even if it wasn't the FCC wouldn't allow it to go out over the air. Had it been possible to transmit, and had the FCC given it its blessing, it would have destroyed the speakers receiving it.

Smell-O-Vision

In 1953 General Electric exhibited a 3-D image of a rose with scented puffs from an atomizer. They called it Smell-O-Rama. Mike Todd got wind of it and thought it would be a swell idea to make an entirely scented feature. He died before he could bring his idea to fruition but his son, Mike Todd, Jr., carried on in his stead. Todd's *Scent of Mystery* contained 30 odors—garlic, tobacco, coffee, etc.—to correspond with the action on the screen. The smells wafted through the air from a little tube installed in every seat. (A panoramic view of an approaching cow pasture might have added a suspenseful edge.)

It cost about $1,000,000 to make a Smell-O-Vision theater and apparently nobody thought it was worth it, because *Scent of Mystery* was the first and last film to use the process, despite the favorable review given the movie by *The New Yorker*. Then there was Henny Youngman who said he didn't understand the picture because he had a cold.

Spectamation

In Herman Cohen's *Konga* (1961), a gigantic chimpanzee bursts out of a mad doctor's lab in London and makes his way to Big Ben where he stands for a considerable length of time to give the military a chance

Sensurround shakes, rattles, and rolls one poor boob right off his feet in this scene from Earthquake *(Universal, 1974).*

to kill him. These not-so-special effects were accomplished with miniatures and travelling mattes. Producer Cohen said the picture cost him $500,000 but his effects made people believe it cost around three or four million. Actually, it's doubtful that anyone believed he spent the $500,000.

Kerwin Mathews is made to appear gigantic through the miracle of Super Dynamation in The 3 Worlds of Gulliver *(Columbia, 1960).*

Spectarama

Meaningless name given to the effects work (what little there was of it) in AIP's *"X"—The Man with X-Ray Eyes* (1963). Ray Milland played the title character and from time to time the audience is supposed to see what he sees but it was a very inexpensive movie and the special effects simply weren't there. "The picture turned out reasonably well," said producer-director Roger Corman, "but I think, when finished, it did suffer from that. We did the best we could. To show a man seeing through a building I photographed buildings that were in various stages of construction, on the basis he could see through the outer skin — which was a reasonable cheat — but it still was a cheat."

Super Dynamation

Used in the motion picture *The 3 Worlds of Gulliver* (1960). See: Dynamation.

Vitamotion

"The film process newer than tomorrow!" claimed the advertisements for *Sword and the Dragon* (1960) but there really isn't a clue given as to what Vitamotion is. Perhaps it was the name of the company that supplied the 65 motors that supposedly animated the full-size, three-headed dragon. This spectacular Russian film was completed in 1956 but wasn't released in America until the Italian muscleman movies opened the market.

Six

Witch Deflectors
and Fear Flashers

*I really feel that there is no showmanship to speak of in
Hollywood today. I think it's an ingredient that is sadly
missing from our American scene—the fun of exploitation.* — **William Castle, Producer-Director**

A few decades ago practically every store in town proudly displayed a sign that read: WE GIVE S&H GREEN STAMPS. The sign was
often larger than the name of the store displaying it, the stamps became
that popular. They were the equivalent of the coupons some tobacco
companies used to give with their cigarettes. For every dollar spent the
customer got a stamp. The stamps were pasted in books and when the
books were full they were taken to an S&H Redemption Center and
traded for a piece of merchandise—a toaster or camera or whatever.
After a while if a store didn't give Green Stamps they'd better jolly well
give Blue Chip Stamps or nobody shopped there. But when you went

If you saw this horror combination you were given Black Stamps. Unfortunately, there was no Black Stamp redemption center.

to see *The Curse of the Mummy's Tomb* and *The Gorgon* (1964) you got Black Stamps. And there was no redemption center.

During the 1940s theaters used to give away dishes or play Keno (a variation of Bingo) for cash, or both, to entice customers. For some reason there was a resurgence of this giveaway philosophy in the 1960s, only by then the studios were rarely offering anything quite as useful as dishes. If you saw Columbia's *The H Man* (1959), you were given a highly compressed sponge, die-cut in the shape of a man with this imprint: DIP "THE H MAN" IN WATER ... *AND WATCH OUT*.

To promote *Witchcraft* (1964), Fox offered plastic, day-glo "Witch Deflectors," the only way to escape the horror on the screen. For their

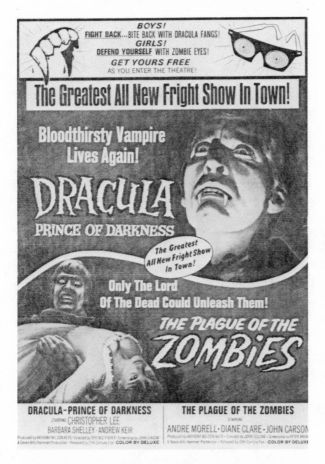

The 1960s was the decade of the giveaways. (Top) Zombie eyes and Dracula fangs were offered to patrons of Dracula, Prince of Darkness *and* Plague of the Zombies *(20th Century–Fox, 1966). (Bottom) The Witch Deflector for* Witchcraft *(20th Century–Fox, 1964).*

combination program of *Dracula, Prince of Darkness* and *Plague of the Zombies* (1966), Fox gave Dracula fangs to the male customers and Zombie eyes to the females. (Nonparticipating exhibitors were horrified to note that all of their customers appeared to be wearing Zombie eyes at the end of the program.) Everyone was expected to don a beard (blue for the boys and pink for the ladies) for screenings of *Rasputin — the Mad Monk* (1966) which was supposed to protect the wearer from the forces of evil. At the very least it offered a disguise for anyone who might have wanted to slip out of the theater without being recognized.

This business of protecting customers started with William Castle's insurance policy idea for *Macabre* and was in full bloom ten years later. American International handed out little envelopes with salt and iron "to ward off the curse of any witch" for their *Burn Witch, Burn* (1962) and as an extra precaution suggested a recital of the following "ancient" incantation featured in the film's "protective prologue": "O, creator of Hecate, Demkina, Marduk's Messenger . . . tem-khepera, khnemu . . . Beelzebub in the netherworld . . . Satan in Gehenna . . . Controller of the seven thousand and seven curses and talismans . . . and who is known to obedient disciples as Gangida . . . hold all your powers and those of your do-bidders . . . and their familiars . . . and cast a protecting shield above those gathered present. Pull back from airy bodies those vested with evil . . . grant, o magnificent one, no harm from the spells about to be witnessed. Direct them not! This faithful servant begs for Thy favor! Eftir irne-zet! Now with a free mind and a protected soul, we ask you to enjoy *Burn Witch, Burn!*"

Before you could see Filmgroup's *Dementia 13* (1963) you had to take the following test:

1. Have you ever spoken aloud to yourself in a mirror? (The answer is YES. Everyone has experienced this behavior. To be able to admit your behavior as it is, is a sign of emotional stability.)

2. Do you always think carefully before you speak? (The answer is NO. Excessive caution like excessive recklessness may indicate your mind is preoccupied with fear of becoming involved in a situation dangerous to your security.)

3. Have you ever raised your hand in anger to a close relative? (The answer is YES. Almost everyone has "lost control" once in a while. It is the teakettle that is *prevented* from letting off steam that is in danger of exploding.)

4. Do you believe yourself to be sincere although others may not be? (The answer is YES. Everyone believes himself to be "sincere." It

Before you could see Dementia 13, *you had to take their D-13 test
(Filmgroup/American International, 1963).*

is always the other fellow who is insincere. A normal method of transfer-ring guilt feelings is to project them onto others.)

5. Were you ever involved in what passed for an accident but which you really purposely caused? (The answer is NO. Unresolved guilt feelings seek expression in self-punishment which may result in anti-social or other unacceptable behavior.)

6. Have you ever been seriously depressed to the point of con-sidering suicide? (The answer is YES. Everyone has been depressed and everyone has considered suicide at sometime or another. Failure to ap-preciate these feelings in yourself may be a danger.)

7. Do you feel that as a child you were rejected by one or both of your parents? (The answer is YES. All children are occasionally rejected by their parents. Persons unable to appreciate their parents as human beings with virtues and vices not dissimilar to their own have not fully matured. Continuance of a relationship in which unrealistic virtues are heaped on parents may result in mental illness evidenced by departures from reality.)

8. Did you ever do anything seriously wrong for which you felt little or no guilt? (The answer is NO. It is normal to feel guilty when you do something *you* feel is seriously wrong. A complete absence of a con-science may be an indication of a psychopathic personality.)

9. Has your general state of mental health deteriorated over the years? (The answer is NO. One's mental defenses and ability to deal suc-cessfully with problems should improve with knowledge and ex-perience. If your evaluation of yourself is progressively deteriorating, you need to see your doctor.)

10. Death by drowning in a pond is best described by the word "exciting." (The answer is NO. Actions described as "exciting" fre-quently indicate the person may be drawn toward the activity by a sub-conscious desire.)

11. Have you ever actually attempted suicide or purposely tried to injure a friend? (The answer is NO. Even an actual suicide attempt dur-ing an emotional crisis is not necessarily an indication of mental illness. It may mean subconscious unresolved violence.)

12. The most effective way of settling a dispute is with one quick stroke of the axe to your adversary's head? (The answer is NO. While effective, one who prefers an anti-social act of such violence may be nursing subconscious homicidal tendencies.)

13. Have you ever been hospitalized in a locked mental ward, sanitarium, rest home, or other facility for treatment of mental illness? (The answer is NO. Persons who have recovered from mental illness should be especially careful to avoid possible harmful suggestions.)

Dementia 13 *was only one of the many films to employ tests as a means of daring its audience into the theater. Here's one for William Castle's* The Night Walker *(Universal, 1964).*

This test was designed by Dr. William J. Bryan, Jr., for the purpose of weeding out viewers who might be adversely affected by the movie. If you want to know where you stand score 2 points for each answer in which you lied; 1 point for each truthful answer and 3 points if your answer to number 13 was YES. If your score is more than 10 don't see the movie. If you scored more than 6 points you might need a mental health examination. You surely need one if you bothered to take the test.

THE EXPLOITATION SHOW

WITH THE "BUILT IN"

Follow through on this

1-2-3 SHOCK CAMPAIGN

STEP

HERALD-THROWAWAY AND EYE-SHIELD PROTECTOR

ADVANCE DISTRIBUTION THROWAWAY

STEP NUMBER ONE INVOLVES THE CAREFUL DIS-TRIBUTION OF THE HERALD, REPRODUCED AT LEFT, AND MEASURING 8½ x 5½ INCHES WITH TWO INCHES BLANK AT BOTTOM TO ALLOW FOR THEA-TRE IMPRINT.

THIS THROWAWAY SHOULD BE DISTRIBUTED AS EFFECTIVELY AS POSSIBLE ON THE LOCAL LEVEL, PERHAPS OUTFITTING AN USHER IN FRANKENSTEIN OUTFIT RENTED FROM LOCAL COSTUMER AND HAV-ING HIM TOUR THE CITY'S BUSY SPOTS.

EYE-SHIELD

THE SPECIAL EYE-SHIELD PROTECTOR ALSO RE-PRODUCED IN HERALD, HAS BEEN MANUFACTURED IN A GREEN-TINTED CELLULOID SUBSTANCE, MEAS-URES 3 x 5 INCHES AND IS DISTRIBUTED TO YOUR PATRONS AS THEY ENTER YOUR THEATRE.

NOTE: THIS THROWAWAY HERALD IS TO BE MADE ON THE LOCAL LEVEL. USE THE TEASER AD MAT SHOWN IN AD SECTION. EYE-SHIELDS CAN BE OR-DERED FROM YOUR NEAREST ALLIED ARTISTS EX-CHANGE.

Allied Artists provided not just helpful hints but products for provincial ballyhooers with its release Frankenstein Meets the Space Monster *(1965); its "space shield eye-protector" protects against the "high intensity cobalt rays that glow from the screen . . . ."*

The director of the Advertising Code Administration did not find Dr. Bryan's test amusing, fearing that it endorsed the idea that movies *could* cause crime. A similar but far less pretentious test was devised for

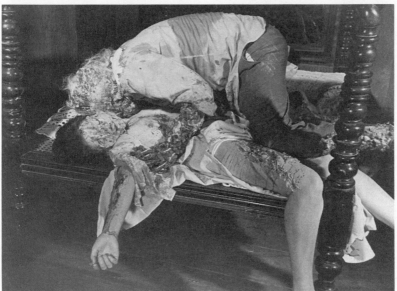

Two diverse love scenes from The Mad Doctor of Blood Island *which asked its audience to drink green blood to get them in the mood for love. (Top)* John Ashley and Angelique Pettijohn *seem to be having a good time. (Bottom)* It appears *that things have gotten out of hand. (Hemisphere, 1969.)*

This self-contained Fear Flasher unit is included in the "Package of Horror" kit. It operates on batteries, gives off a repeating red light signal when started. Unit can be attached to 'HORRORS' 40 by 60, to door panels, to theatre wall, or can be put on display in store windows or elsewhere.

The Fear Flasher, used in connection with the Horror Horn, kept people awake during Chamber of Horrors *(Warner Bros., 1966).*

Columbia's *Berserk* (1967). There were five questions on display in the lobby of the theater. If you answered YES to more than three of the questions you saw the picture at your own risk, which, I might add, you did regardless of your answers.

People seeing United Artists' *The Lost Missile* (1958) were asked to wear "Shock Tags." Anyone shocked into a comatose state would get a free ride home in a limousine. And the "Space Shield Eye Protector" that you got when you saw *Frankenstein Meets the Space Monster* (1965) would save you from being abducted into outer space.

Actor-producer John Ashley made a series of horror films in the

(Opposite) *Warning bells alerted viewers that something disgusting was about to be shown in* Terror Is a Man *(Valiant Films, 1959) and* Cannibal Girls *(American International, 1972).*

Philippines and three of them sported gimmick giveaways. The first was *Brides of Blood* (1968 — also known as *Grave Desires* and *Island of Living Horror*) which offered plastic wedding rings to its female customers. During the prologue of *The Mad Doctor of Blood Island* (1969 — also known as *Tomb of the Living Dead*) the audience was asked to drink the "green blood" they'd been given as they entered the theater which was supposed to act as an aphrodisiac. (I don't know about you but if it was romance I was after, it would never occur to me to look for it in a horror picture.) More thoughtful, and more necessary, were the survival kits, with barf bags, distributed for *Beast of Blood* (1970 — also known as *Beast of the Dead*). According to Ashley, it was pretty gruesome.

"We were able to do things over there you just couldn't do here," he said, referring to the fact that the picture was shot in the Philippines. "For example, we would show an insert of a knife going into a body. Here you'd have to fake it. There, we would buy a pig and shave its skin and put body makeup over its stomach and just take the knife and plunge it in. Of course, the pig was doped up so he didn't feel a thing. I did one other horror film over there that was never released here called *Witchcraft*. In this picture we did an autopsy on a real body. Which was very unique. It was enlightening to me. For a couple of bottles of Johnny Walker we went to the local barrio and got the body of some prisoner who had just been killed in a fight. We were able to film the autopsy. And that whole sequence is in the film. I'm talking about the skull coming off and everything."

Barf bags, or rather "Up-Chuck Cups" were also available to patrons of Europix's combination show *I Dismember Mama* and *The Blood Spattered Bride* (1972) with a guarantee to the exhibitor that the gimmick would "upsurge your boxoffice!" The producers of *Terror Is a Man* (1959 — also known as *Blood Creature*) found a less expensive way to keep the theater clean. Before each gruesome moment a warning bell sounded. The more squeamish members of the audience could cover their eyes. A second bell signaled the "all clear." *Cannibal Girls* (1972) employed the same gimmick but the producers of *Chamber of Horrors* (1966) embellished it. They added "fear flashers" to the "horror horn."

And if intimidation didn't work as a means of luring people into the theater there was always the promise of money. Producer Jack H. Harris offered a million bucks to anyone who could duplicate the actions of the title character in his *4-D Man* (1959). Which meant a person had to walk through wooden doors, become part of a galvanized, electrical

If you could pass through a wall like Robert Lansing here you could make a smooth $1 million from producer Jack H. Harris. (From 4-D Man, *Universal-International, 1959.)*

fence, pass through the wall of an atomic reactor, withstand atomic bombardments, and walk through solid steel. Anyone that could do all of that would hardly be grubbing for bucks from Harris. But if you were thinking of trying it, forget it. The offer expired in November of 1961. Harris wasn't taking any chances.

Less sure of themselves than Harris, Fox offered a paltry $100 to anyone who could prove the events in *The Fly* (1958) couldn't happen. And if you could prove that the monster in UA's *It! The Terror from Beyond Space* wasn't actually on Mars you got a free trip to that planet on the first commercially scheduled flight. There may have been an expiration date on that one too.

Cash being in short supply, Allied Artists suggested their exhibitors give away flower seeds for their release of *The Day of the Triffids* (1963). Only they weren't even going to supply the seeds. "Suggest that you have a quantity of open end envelopes (3" x 5½") printed, using the 'Triffid Seeds' copy word for word," the publicity department told their exhibitors. The copy was as follows:

TRIFFID SEEDS

(Triffidus Celestus)

These seeds are reported to be for one of the rarest plants ever known. They are believed to have been brought to earth on meteorites.

WARNING! Under *certain conditions* the Triffid plant will grow to tremendous heights, bigger than a man, and become a carnivorous destroyer whose attack is deadly to all living things. This occurs especially when certain cosmic influences come into play, as when the earth passes through a

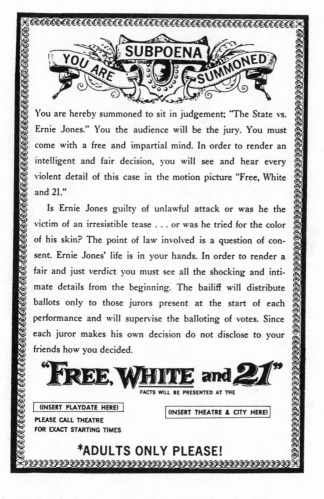

dense cloud of meteorites. There is no known defense or an-
tidote for an attack by a Triffid.

Beware of THE DAY OF THE TRIFFIDS! Plant these
seeds at your own risk. Watch the plants' growth carefully . . . if they show carnivorous tendencies they should be
immediately destroyed!

The publicity department suggested sunflower seeds dyed green.
Nobody bothered. The same gimmick was used for Paramount's *Torture
Garden* (1967).

One of the most elaborate stunts was cooked up by American International for their *Free, White and 21* (1963). Taking a cue from Bill

Castle's Punishment Poll idea, bogus subpoenas were passed out a few weeks ahead of the movie's playdate, ordering people to come and decide the guilt or innocence of the defendant in the story. At the theater patrons were handed ballots. The film's trial sequences were played as if the audience was the jury. The action of the film was stopped to give the ushers time to collect the ballots. The theater manager then announced "The trial of Ernie Jones is now ready for continuance. Will the jurors please return to their seats in the jury box." As payment for their service, three-inch long, wood-colored plastic gavels inscribed "I served on the *Free, White and 21* jury" were given away by the more generous exhibitors.

Not long ago the master of poor taste, John Waters, made a movie called *Polyester* (1981) which was touted as the first film in Odorama. It was a variation on Smell-O-Vision only instead of piping odors into the theater everyone was given a scratch-and-sniff card with 8 or 10 unpleasant odors. Whatever happened to Green Stamps?

Seven

16 Cameras! 1,600 Camels!

*"Over-Exposed!" Starring Cleo Moore! As the girl who
shot her way to the top! With a camera! Curves! And
no conscience!"*
—Radio Spot for Over-Exposed

The Cozy was located in downtown Los Angeles, at the northern
end of Broadway and the butt end of affluence. The marquee was tiny,
scarcely large enough for two titles, and The Cozy ran three features,
four on weekends. All titles therefore had to be distilled, which created
some interesting interpretations. One week it proudly boasted *Peace
and War*. It was hardly cause for concern. It didn't matter what was on
the marquee. The Cozy offered an alternative to people who couldn't
afford a place to stay. It was shelter for fifty cents, from nine in the morning to well after midnight. The movies ran nonstop, which mercifully
kept the auditorium in darkness. People slept on the concrete floor.
Others wrapped like snakes around the dividers and slept on the hard

wooden chairs. Everything was filthy. The only fresh air came from the large crack in the ceiling near the top of the screen. Equally depressing was the sign outside next to the entrance that read "Make it a Cozy habit." Yet, meticulously displayed for every attraction was a poster and fifteen or twenty 8 by 10 inch photographs. Now that's showmanship.

Before TV became the primary selling ground of motion pictures, studios and exhibitors worked hand in hand to sell a film, with the help of the artists who designed the advertising campaigns. Exhibitors were given pressbooks which contained newspaper advertising and promotional stunts. The stunts were often elaborate, way beyond hanging a few posters and stills. Exhibitors were asked to overhaul their lobbies to match the theme of their attraction and to orchestrate incredible cooperative advertising stunts that often involved entire cities. Just how often these suggestions were taken to heart remains a mystery but many of the schemes should prove interesting reading. (When it doesn't I trust that the publisher's Complete-O—see the Preface—will kick into gear.)

Quite often exhibitors were given a boost by some pre-selling by the studios. One way to accomplish this was to have an actor or actress endorse a product like Lux Toilet Soap, the way Jean Arthur did for *You Can't Take It with You* (1938). The performer plugs the product and the product plugs the movie. *You Can't Take It with You* is one of the best examples of pre-selling and co-op advertising stunts, made more intriguing because it was a case where the movie sold itself. It had a popular cast, a popular director, and was based on a popular play. It was a studio executive's dream. Yet Columbia bent over backwards to promote it further.

Jean Arthur wasn't the only member of the cast to get involved with co-op advertising. Ann Miller was asked to say a good word about Jergens Lotion and Duart Permanent waves. When the movie opened at the Radio City Music Hall in New York, the Mutual Savings Banks of Manhattan, Bronx, and Westchester ran a full page newspaper ad that featured Lionel Barrymore reminding people, "You can't take it with you, so why not save to spend?" Color enlargements of that ad were on display in all of the banks, a campaign that could easily be altered to fit any bank or savings and loan. And Spring Byington, who played a character in the film who wrote plays because someone delivered a typewriter to her home by mistake, appeared in an ad for a Remington Noiseless Typewriter. The ad read: "Spring Byington Found Her Remington So Irresistible—She Just Had to Write a Play!"

"YOU CAN'T TAKE IT WITH YOU"

says Lionel Barrymore

"So why not save to spend ?"

"In my latest Columbia picture, Frank Capra's *You Can't Take It With You*, now playing at the Radio City Music Hall, Grandpa Vanderhof, the

character I portray, had one grand philosophy. When he felt he had saved up enough money, he stopped work and began to enjoy the better

things in life He was the happiest man I've ever heard of. For he did exactly as he pleased He owned his own home, collected stamps, helped

people, made friends. And how did he do it? Well, he must have worked very hard when he was young and saved his money little by little "

You, too, can enjoy the better things in life. Put a few dollars in your nearest *mutual* Savings Bank every pay-day. In no time at all, you will have the cash to get the things *you* want. *Mutual* Savings Banks are operated solely for the benefit of depositors. There are no stocks nor stockholders

The mutual

All Savings Banks in New York State are mutual

SAVINGS BANKS

of Manhattan, Bronx and Westchester

Co-op advertising split the cost of promotion.

Solo ads for the film appeared in 19 fan magazines with a circulation of 25,000,000 readers. But that wasn't enough. Exhibitors were asked to recruit everyone from the Chamber of Commerce to the clergy to help sell the picture. Columbia's publicity department cooked up a slogan — "Spend Wisely for Better Living — You Can't Take It with You" — and wanted exhibitors to use it as a challenge. A challenge to consumers everywhere to spend until their brains fell out. And, of course, to see the movie while they were at it.

The whole plan was mapped out for the exhibitors. They were given a calendar to follow that began three weeks prior to the opening date. One of the activities was something called "Better Living Week."

To get "Better Living Week" underway, an exhibitor had to convince a local mayor that the stunt would be a mutually beneficial one. The mayor then issued the following statement:

"We are faced with a challenge!

"A family is coming to town, shouting at us:

"'We know how to enjoy life — do you?'

"I have been privileged to meet these life-loving, fun-loving folk, and next week you will meet them, Grandpa Vanderhof and his household. While they are here I am calling on the people of this city to answer their challenge by participating in 'Better Living Week.' It seems that once Grandpa Vanderhof learned that 'You Can't Take It with You,' and since that time he and his family have been learning how to live and how to use what they had rather than hoard more than they could ever hope to use. Our slogan will be: 'Spend wisely for better living — you can't take it with you.'

"Let us all get into the spirit of "Better Living Week" — let us realize that every dollar wisely spent means better living all around. It means that you will enjoy your purchase and that some one else in turn will be enabled to purchase something he needs. Wealth must circulate and re-circulate to make more jobs and buy more things. After all, you can't take it with you, but you can enjoy the things money will buy. Buy now, and enable others to buy!

"'Better Living Week' will be a week for merchant and consumer to get together. Merchants will cooperate by showing all the modern, wonderful new things that make for better living! And today's prices represent real bargains, so that the consumer can't help but cooperate.

"On behalf of this city, I welcome Grandpa Vanderhof and his family and their heart-warming story, 'You Can't Take It with You.'

I welcome the challenge they bring, a challenge which will answer to the credit of the people of this city during 'Better Living Week'."

It was assumed that any opportunity to spur business would appeal to the Chamber of Commerce who would, in turn, help the exhibitor with a special dinner to launch the campaign. Following the dinner there would be a private screening of the movie.

Of course a campaign that sanctioned a spending spree meant merchants would be spending more money for advertising and no "wide-awake newspaper advertising manager" could ignore the opportunity to promote special ads. And the drive itself would be news. Imagine, a motion picture that pointed the way to a better living, "not by showing lavish luxuries we cannot afford, but the things within reach of all, that make life so worth living for any family!" Naturally, with the mayor, the Chamber of Commerce, and the newspapers joining forces, the merchants couldn't afford to stay out of the parade. After all, "one of the most compelling sales slogans ever conceived" was any merchant's for the asking. With the slogan in every window in town and on banners across the city's busiest streets, how could anyone lose?

The Hotel Astor in New York City gave Columbia 100,000 postcards with a hand-written message printed on the back: "Having a nice visit here at Hotel Astor. Just saw Frank Capra's 'You Can't Take It with You.' A marvelous picture! Don't miss it when it comes to town. Sincerely, Alice."

But having the Hotel Astor, and the mayor and the Chamber of Commerce and the newspapers and every merchant in town promoting the movie still wasn't enough. Columbia wanted God on their side and to that end suggested the following letter be sent to all the clergymen:

"Dear Dr. Smith:

"To paraphrase a famous song 'the good things in life are rare'—and all the more precious for their rarity. That is why we are taking such pride in 'You Can't Take with You,' which we hope you will see and enjoy as much as we have. We could, if we so desired, go into fervent praise for the manner in which Director Frank Capra has turned the Pulitzer Prize play by Georgy S. Kaufman and Moss Hart into a warm, human and vital screen document, replete with a philosophy of life that should commend itself to all who are bewildered by a strife-torn, money-harassed world.

"In Matthew we read that 'it is easier for a camel to go through the eye of a needle, than for a rich man to enter into the kingdom of God.'

Mr. Capra emphasizes this so effectively, so richly, so humanly that we feel the need of urging you to see 'You Can't Take It with You,' in the hope that you in turn, will help carry the message of the film to your congregation. 'You Can't Take It with You' is a motion picture we are proud to present. We are proud of the fact that Columbia Pictures has chosen us to offer this film to the citizens of . . . . and we sincerely hope that you will share our pride by seeing 'You Can't Take It with You.' When you do, we are confident that you will find in it a source and inspiration for an important message to those who have come to lean heavily upon your advice and help.

"Sincerely, (Signed) Theatre Mgr."

A similar plot was hatched by 20th Century–Fox to bamboozle entire cities into promoting *The Story of Alexander Graham Bell* (1939). Instead of celebrating a spending spree, Fox wanted to toast the progress that had been made since the invention of the telephone. Somehow the studio managed to wangle two rather prestigious premieres for the picture — on the West Coast at the Golden Gate International Exposition, and at Constitution Hall in Washington, D.C., on the East Coast (sponsored by the National Geographic Society no less). With such an auspicious debut, and considering the subject of the film, Fox probably figured they had something legitimate for people to rally around. Again they wanted the Mayor to set the ball rolling, backed by a committee of representatives from civic organizations, women's clubs, municipal officials and newspapers. Of course, the telephone would play a big part in this selling campaign. Exhibitors were urged to try any or all of the following suggestions:

"Locate the first telephone subscriber in your town. Generally this would be telephone number 1. An interview should be good for some great human interest copy. If this is not feasible you still might interest your paper in a feature story on the colorful local angle of the town when the telephone was an amazing new invention.

"If you have a local [Walter] Winchell you might interest him in the idea of a column based on the old multiple party line. You've probably heard of, and may remember, the old style party line with 6 to 10 subscribers which gave your phone conversations as much privacy as a gold-fish. You may also remember how one surreptitiously removed their receiver to listen when the signal bell definitely indicated the call for the Jones family down the line! There's no dearth of material for such a column which can result in a very worthwhile plug for the picture.

"Locate some of the early telephone operators. The resultant interviews should net some very fine publicity in the way of feature stories regarding the use of the telephone. Thrilling, exciting and humorous anecdotes should be plentiful. The local angle can be made very colorful with former prominent personalities, civic events and local happenings in which the telephone played an important part.

"'Doodling,' the drawing of odd and eccentric designs on scrap paper while telephoning, probably rivals baseball as our national pastime. A contest based on 'doodling' should attract a multitude of contestants. Perhaps you could get the mayor and other prominent local folks, if they are devotees of the hobby, to submit samples of their handiwork for lobby display or as illustration if you conduct the contest in conjunction with a newspaper.

"A contest for your front or newspaper could be based on the local phone directory. Take pages at random and circle numbers. Those encircled on the pages displayed on your front, could be awarded guest tickets. If run as a newspaper contest add a short letter as an additional requirement and check with your local phone company before starting the contest.

"Use your local phone directory for a mailing list to which you can direct your selling appeal to the users of phone service. Lead off with this copy on the mailing piece which of course will include picture art and billing: " . . . . . . (write in phone number). Did you know that the miraculous invention of the telephone which you use daily was inspired by a great love? See the thrilling, romantic drama behind this great achievement that symbolizes the tradition of America! See America's most thrilling story!

"You could start a chain phone campaign by asking each member of your staff to call five friends and give them a spiel about the picture. In turn each of the five called could be asked to call five more. This chain idea might work out better for a group of women's clubs. If you can arrange a screening for their officers you might ask them to arrange a chain campaign among their members.

"Post cards in public places that have phone booths. These cards can tie-up with the merchant on a courtesy angle. Copy might be: 'For Your Convenience! You Will Find Telephone Booths at the Rear of the Store. Change Gladly Made. See America's Most Thrilling Story! The Romance of the Invention of the Telephone!'"

If all of that wasn't enough for the exhibitor to contend with he was also expected to find an old switchboard (or have a reasonable facsimile made) and have it converted into a public address system. Above the switchboard he was supposed to display some "romantic art" from the movie along with a banner that read: "1878! When you talked through the receiver! When the 'hello girls' were 'hello boys'! A great miracle had been wrought out of the dreams and struggles, love and achievement of Alexander Graham Bell!" An usher, dressed in a costume of the period, gave "intimate spiels" over the P.A. system to people passing by.

In movie history there may be nothing that tops the bonus pre-selling campaign that Columbia got by making *The Fuller Brush Man* (1948). Suddenly there were 7000 free door-to-door salesmen at their disposal. Howard Fuller, the president of the Fuller Brush Company, got behind the film 100 percent. He gave Columbia thousands of free brushes for theaters across the country to give away. The salesmen were given matchbooks and door hangers plugging the picture.

The urge to link stunts to film titles often led the more literal-minded publicist to suggest something foolish. It must have been a bachelor in Columbia's employ who thought having children throw rubber balls at paper saucers was a good way to promote the studio's *Earth vs. the Flying Saucers* (1956). Now and then the result of this penchant for the obvious led the publicist away from the foolish to the grotesque, as was the case of *Monkey on My Back* (1957), the biography of fighter Barney Ross who became addicted to narcotics. And there was the equally tasteful stunt suggested by Universal to promote *The Girl in the Kremlin* (1957). The film raised the question "Is Stalin Alive?" So while the movie was in production, actor Maurice Manson strolled through the streets of New York in his Red Army uniform, looking very much like Joseph Stalin. A couple of policemen were on hand in case there was trouble but the whole business proved uneventful. Either no one noticed or they simply didn't care. Which was the beauty of the stunt according to Universal. It made a good newspaper story "whether Stalin strolling through the streets creates no stir or whether an incipient riot is started."

It's interesting to see how some of the classic films were sold. Naturally once a film becomes a classic it more or less sells itself but before that happens it's just another piece of merchandise, subject to the same hard sell approach as any other film. For starters, take a look at the campaign for *Psycho* (1960) which was personally supervised by Alfred Hitchcock himself. The cherubic director insisted that the

*The advertisements for 12 Angry Men urged audiences to see it from the begin-
ning. Here Lee J. Cobb demonstrates how the boy on trial stabbed his father.
Henry Fonda hopes it's only a demonstration (United Artists, 1957).*

exhibitors adopt a policy of secrecy about the story and that no one be
allowed to enter the theater after the start of each performance.

Even in 1960 this wasn't exactly a fresh idea. Four years earlier the
ads for *12 Angry Men* (1957) read "Please see it from the beginning!" And
the idea was used long before that film. All the way back to the silent
era I would suspect. But Hitchcock wasn't suggesting that people see
his picture from the beginning, he was demanding it. Some exhibitors
expressed concern about chasing customers away but Hitchcock had
some opening playdates to point to as evidence that his restricted
seating policy was paying off. And after a few months Paramount's
distribution branches began receiving unsolicited testimonials from
grateful showmen. Here are some examples:

HOW THRILLING, HOW EXCITING, AFTER MY MANY YEARS IN ALL
TYPES AND KINDS OF SHOWMANSHIP ACTIVITIES NEVER HAVE I HAD

MORE PLEASURE THAN IN PARTICIPATING WITH YOU AND THE
PARAMOUNT GANG IN THE RECORD BREAKING SHOWMANSHIP
ENGAGEMENTS OF PSYCHO AT OUR DEMILLE AND BARONET
THEATRES. MERCHANDISING ADVERTISING AND PROMOTIONAL
CAMPAIGN HAS PULLED THE STOP FOR NEW YORK AND I AM SURE
WILL DO LIKE-WISE FOR THE REST OF THE COUNTRY. AGAIN MY
CONGRATULATIONS TO WHAT I KNOW WILL BE A LONG RECORD
SHATTERING ENGAGEMENT PSYCHO IS HITCHCOCKS MOST EX-
CITING SO FAR. — WALTER READE JR.

PSYCHO POLICY PAYING OFF TO FANTASTIC OPENING DAY AT AR-
CADIA TOPPING BY FAR LAST YEAR'S BIGGEST MONEY WINNER.
ALL EXHIBITORS SHOULD REALIZE YOUR PSYCHO POLICY IS A
MUST. BEST REGARDS. — MERT AND BEN SHAPIRO.

WE ARE ALL THRILLED WITH THE RESULTS OF THE HITCH-
COCK CAMPAIGN. IT IS REALLY BALLYHOO SHOWMANSHIP
WHICH THE PUBLIC ENJOYS. THE PEOPLE LOVE PSYCHO BUT
THEY ALSO LIKE THE MANNER IN WHICH IT IS PRESENTED. WE
WILL CONTINUE TO ADHERE TO THE OVERALL POLICY DURING
THE ENTIRE ENGAGEMENT. WE FEEL THAT IF EXHIBITORS PUR-
SUE THIS POLICY NATIONALLY IT WILL BE AS SUCCESSFUL AS IT
IS AT THE WOODS THEATRE. KINDEST REGARDS. — EDWIN
SILVERMAN.

I ADMIRE THE COURAGE OF PARAMOUNT PICTURES IN IN-
AUGURATING THE NEW ADVERTISING SALES ANGLE WITH
PSYCHO. SINCE THE PHENOMENAL SUCCESS WITH THE WAY IT
HAS CAUGHT ON IN BOSTON I AM THOROUGHLY CONVINCED
THAT THIS SHOW MUST BE SEEN FROM THE BEGINNING WITH
THE NEW POLICY MAINTAINED. THE BUSINESS IS MOST GRATIFY-
ING. I KNOW WE WILL SKYROCKET TO NEW HIGH GROSSES IN
NEW ENGLAND. THANKS FOR NEW LIFE. KEEP THEM COMING.
REGARDS. — BOB STERNBURG.

PSYCHO OPENING WEDNESDAY JULY 6TH BRUNSWICK DRIVE IN
NEW BRUNSWICK NJ BIGGEST SINGLE DAY BUSINESS INCLUDING
SATURDAY, SUNDAY, AND HOLIDAY IN THEATRE'S 10 YEAR
HISTORY. CAR CAPACITY REACHED 30 MINUTES BEFORE FIRST

Director Alfred Hitchcock, 1961.

SHOWING. POLICY OF NO ADMITTANCE AFTER FEATURE STARTS
TREMENDOUS SUCCESS. ENTIRE PARKING AREA FRONT OF BOX
OFFICE FULL 45 MINUTES BEFORE END OF FIRST SHOWING.
CARS WERE BACKED UP THREE MILES ON RTE 1 AND ONLY
REFUSAL OF STATE POLICE TO ALLOW CONTINUANCE OF SAME
ON THIS MAIN ARTERY PREVENTED OUR HAVING CAR CAPACITY
FOR SECOND SHOW. HOWEVER WE ARE CERTAIN ALL THOSE
TURNED AWAY WILL BE BACK. LOOKING FORWARD TO EVEN
MORE SENSATIONAL BUSINESS REST OF ENGAGEMENT PLUS
HOLD OVER AS WORD OF MOUTH TERRIFIC. CAN'T WAIT TO BOOK
PSYCHO IN OUR OTHER DRIVE IN. — HARRY AND JOSEPH
APPLEMAN.

For those unfortunates who had to wait in line, Hitch prepared a number of entertaining recordings to smooth the ruffled feathers of the more impatient members in line. Exhibitors had five of these recordings to choose from:

Version 1. "Greetings, ladies and gentlemen. This disembodied voice which you hear belongs to Alfred Hitchcock. I wish to warn you about the motion picture you are about to see at this theatre. It is called *Psycho* and is a picture which was designed to be as terrifying and shocking as possible, from start to finish. In view of this, I have suggested that *Psycho* be seen from the beginning. In fact, this is more than a suggestion, it is required. As has been announced, no one is being admitted to the theatre after the start of each performance of *Psycho*. Although I do apologize for any inconvenience, the point of all this, of course, is to help you enjoy *Psycho* more. You see, we like you and want you to be happy. What more can I say?"

Version 2. "This is Alfred Hitchcock. We trust that the presence of a special policeman throughout the current engagement of *Psycho* will not prove annoying or frightening. Personally, they scare me to death.

"Actually, he merely represents the theatre management who have been instructed to make certain that no one is seated after the picture begins. You will thus be assured of the full, start-to-finish enjoyment of . . . [etc.]."

Version 3. "This voice you hear is Alfred Hitchcock,—so is this apology. Please forgive me for denying you the immediate comfort of those plush reclining seats but you won't enjoy them, really, if you see *Psycho* from the middle, or near the end, or at any time except that at which it actually begins. We won't allow you to cheat yourself. Every theatre manager everywhere, has been instructed to admit no one . . . [etc.]."

Version 4. "This is Alfred Hitchcock. Having lived with *Psycho* since it was a gleam in my camera's eye, I now exercise my parental rights in revealing a number of significant facts about this well . . . eh . . . uh . . . slightly extraordinary entertainment.

"First of all, I must warn you that *Psycho* was designed to be as terrifying as possible. Do not, however, heed the false rumor that it will frighten the moviegoer speechless. We do want you to tell your friends to come too . . . [etc.]."

Version 5. "How do you do, ladies and gentlemen. This is Alfred

Hitchcock. I must apologize for inconveniencing you in this way. However, this queuing up and standing about is good for you. It will make you appreciate the seats inside. It will also make you appreciate *Psycho*. You see, *Psycho* is most enjoyable when viewed beginning at the beginning and proceeding to the end. I realize this is a revolutionary concept but we have discovered that *Psycho* is unlike most motion pictures and does not improve when run backwards . . . [etc.]."

Hitch also had some handy tips on how to handle those lines. And some instructions to the projectionist about keeping the theater dark for 30 seconds after the movie was over. "Never, never, never will I permit *Psycho* to be followed immediately by a short subject or newsreel," said the director, who believed that 30 seconds of Stygian blackness would indelibly engrave the suspense of the movie into the minds of his audience. Hitch left nothing to the exhibitor's imagination.

Going a little further back in time we'll take a look at another Paramount film classic, *The Lost Weekend* (1945), to see how it was handled. As it was based on a best-selling book by Charles Jackson, which had been condensed in *Coronet* magazine (read by some 2½ million subscribers), and serialized by King Features in newspapers across the country, the movie had been pretty well presold. And because of the sensitive nature of the material (a grim look at the life of an alcoholic), the publicity department more or less decided to let the critics do their talking for them. The only thing left for the exhibitor to do was to contact the various organizations in his community—women's clubs, Kiwanis Clubs, schools, churches, libraries, etc.—that would likely support a movie that so vividly depicted the evils of alcohol. However, when it came time to ballyhoo another classic of its kind, the supernatural thriller *The Uninvited* (1944), also based on a best-selling novel, Paramount was less dignified in its approach. Although the film of Dorothy Macardle's ghostly yarn was handled with considerable restraint and taste, the publicity boys dipped into the usual bag of tricks that had been used to promote horror movies for years—bloody footprints, horse-drawn wagons dragging bells and chains, records of screams and thunder blasting over loudspeakers, the sort of stuff that William Castle built a career on.

Columbia had a devil of a time selling *The Wild One* (1953), Stanley Kramer's now classic drama of a motorcycle gang that takes over an entire town. Based on a real life incident that took place in a small California town a few years earlier, Kramer's movie outraged a number of

Two faces of Ray Milland. (Top) The alcoholic writer from The Lost Weekend *(1945). (Bottom)* Holding Gail Russell as Ruth Hussey looks on from The Uninvited *(1944). (Both Paramount.)*

people in power before it was even released. The very suggestion that the antisocial behavior depicted in his film could in any way be justified was totally unacceptable to church groups, Congress, the Hayes office, and anyone else concerned with keeping the status quo. And even though the original intentions of its makers were severely diluted, *The Wild One* was still too strong for the taste of the civic-minded. Columbia didn't dare exploit its inflammatory aspects.

The subject matter was completely obliterated from the advertising, which centered on the film's star Marlon Brando. At the time Brando was the hottest property around, having scored strongly in *A Streetcar Named Desire* (1951) with his unique brand of sexuality and earthiness. He quickly earned a bad boy reputation and made himself quite unpopular in an era where leading men were generally about as real as a Ken doll. He was so dynamic the Academy of Motion Picture Arts and Sciences couldn't overlook him no matter how hard they tried and were forced to nominate him for the best actor award for practically every picture in which he appeared for three years but continued to show their animosity against him by handing the award to somebody else until, at last, they just couldn't get away with it any longer and let him win in 1954 for his brilliant performance in *On the Waterfront*. Had it not been for Brando, there would have been nothing to exploit in *The Wild One*.

United Artists had the opposite problem with *Witness for the Prosecution* (1957). They had a lot to sell but weren't altogether sure they had any buyers. The picture had top stars — Tyrone Power, Marlene Dietrich, Charles Laughton — a well-known and respected director, Billy Wilder, and was based on a novel by an extremely popular writer — Agatha Christie. The problem was the audience that would have been interested was home watching television. If the picture was to succeed it had to appeal to the teenage market and the teenagers didn't give a hoot for Tyrone Power and didn't know who Billy Wilder was. So UA had to reach them in another way and they believed local disc jockeys were their best bet. Exhibitors were urged to court deejays to play the title song from the film and offer free tickets to screenings and read the following copy as often as possible:

"Folks, you've been listening to some of the top songs of the week . . . now get ready for the TOP TEN OF A LIFETIME! That's right . . . the top ten is coming, but these top ten are NOT songs . . . they're minutes . . . the most terrific ten minutes of suspense that ever

*John Williams watches Charles Laughton sort through his pills during cross ex-
amination in* **Witness for the Prosecution** *(United Artists, 1957).*

screamed out of a motion picture! I'm talking, of course, about *Witness
for the Prosecution* — I've just seen it, and believe me when I say it's the
most electrifying movie ever made . . . with a sensational ending that
I just can't tell you about. Take my word for it, though, *Witness for the
Prosecution* will leave you gasping and guessing right from the start . . .
and just when you've begun to think that it simply isn't possible for the
suspense to get any greater . . . *Witness for the Prosecution* hits you with
the most spine-tingling ending you've ever experienced! But please,
please promise me you won't tell anyone about the ending!"

United Artists may not have known who to sell *Witness for the
Prosecution* to but Metro-Goldwyn-Mayer knew who buttered their

bread when they made *Forbidden Planet* (1956). Free tickets for children under 12 were in boxes of Quaker Oats, a bonus advertised in 124 Sunday comics, 101 Sunday supplement newspapers, grocery stores, and on television's *Sgt. Preston of the Yukon.*

Exhibitors loved this sort of co-op advertising. A few inexpensive children's tickets were a small price to pay for the kind of exposure their attraction received. Drifting into a not-so-classic motion picture mode, Columbia's *Hellcats of the Navy* (1957) got a boost from General Electric because the film's star, Ronald Reagan, was the host and sometime star of "General Electric Theater" on CBS-TV at the time GE's Frank Hoback sent a letter to all of their appliance distributors to suggest they get together with the exhibitors to promote the movie.

Well aware of the new teenage market, Columbia Pictures made the first movie about the rock 'n' roll phenomenon— *Rock Around the Clock* (1956). All

expenses were spared on this songfest. Columbia knew their target audience would come regardless of how poorly the thing was made just to hear and see the music they loved performed. Exhibitors could put the title on their marquees and relax. But there were plenty of exhibitors who did a lot more than that to insure a full house. In North Carolina the manager of the Center Theatre in Charlotte ran the picture for 36 hours straight, an ordeal that was covered by the local

Arthur Franz, Nancy Davis, and Ronald Reagan in **Hellcats of the Navy** *(Co-lumbia, 1957). Right after this movie Ronnie and Nancy were married.*

papers. Customers who survived were given free coffee and doughnuts. For two days the cashiers at the State Theatre in Cedar Rapids, Ohio, answered the phone with "See you later, alligator." The Paramount Theatre in Des Moines had a juke box in the lobby filled with rock 'n' roll music which patrons could play for free. A local radio station in the city broadcast a dance hall contest which heavily featured Bill Haley records. (Haley was the star of the picture.) At the Paramount that week business could not have been better. Exhibitors worked with disc jockeys in Nebraska, Wisconsin, Oklahoma, Massachusetts, Maine, and Maryland to plug the movie with contests. It was hardly surprising that Columbia released a sequel, *Don't Knock the Rock* (1956), that same year.

Always supporting any efforts by the local exhibitors were the newspaper advertisements and radio announcements. Talented artists designed topnotch advertising campaigns, often for as low as $350. "The studios would have rough screenings of films and sometimes, there'd be as many as seven or eight artists there, every one of them hoping to get

Of all the claims for time spent in making a movie, none could top The Animal World: *2 billion years in the making! (Warner Bros., 1956.)*

the job," recalled Reynold Brown who illustrated over 250 ad campaigns from the early 1950s to the late 1960s. "And even then, there was always a struggle as to whether the final art would be done in New York or Los Angeles" (quoted in "Selling Nightmares," by Stephen Rebello, *Cinefantastique,* vol. 18, no. 2/3, p. 56).

The publicity department usually cluttered the artist's work with outrageous claims. Long before designer jeans made it fashionable to display labels like price tags, movie posters flaunted facts and figures to impress the consumer into buying a ticket. The ads for *Land of the Pharaohs* (1955) boasted "Thousands of actors and extras! 16 CinemaScope cameras! 21,000 workers! 1,600 camels! 104 special built barges! 9,753 players!" And a partridge in a pear tree.

Time was often added to the brew so as to wow the ticket buyer, the implication being that if a film took a long time to make it must be good. Two years for this. Five years for that. And "two billion years in the making" for *The Animal World* (1956): nobody ever topped that.

Often at the top of the poster would be a one-liner that captured the essence of the movie better than its title. Some of these sales pitches are poetic, now and then tasteful, but more often silly and misleading and always—*always*—provocative. In the 1970s, New World Pictures reigned supreme in poster one-liners. "A howling hellcat humping a hot hog on a roaring rampage of revenge!" How's that for a grabber? Or the one for *Caged Heat* (1974): "White hot desires melting cold prison steel." Makes you shiver all over, doesn't it? But wait. Their most perverse line, if not their best, was the one used for *Lady Frankenstein* (1972)—"Only the monster she made could satisfy her strange desires."

It's usually the little companies who supplied the best of these one-liners. The big companies pretend respectability. The little companies are shameless. When pressed, however, the majors'll get down and dirty, exemplified by this little ditty from Warner Bros.' *The Diamond Queen* (1953): "In the heated dark of the Himalayas their love seethed . . . the kiss-starved temptress of the tiger-country and the flame-hearted safari-soldier of fortune!" Not quite as direct as New World's line for *Hollywood Boulevard* (1976), "Where starlets are made!" but it's along the same lines. For sheer poetry however, how about "They'll turn you on from dusk to dawn," the catchline for Centaur's *Graveyard Tramps* (1973).

There are times, however, when the hucksters become complacent and fall back on knee-jerk responses. "Like nothing you have ever seen before!" has adorned more movie ads than McDonald's has burgers. For movies about monsters from the ocean you can't beat "A tidal wave of terror!" This penchant for tapping tried and true phrases often lulled the hucksters into such a tranquil state that they weren't listening to themselves anymore. What other explanation could there be for a line like "Actually filmed in color!" which good old Art Gilmore read with his customary zeal to sell *Curucu, the Beast of the Amazon* (1956). And what about "Every terror *exactly* as filmed!" which is on the ad for *The Black Scorpion* (1957). One can only wonder how it could be any other way.

Radio announcements (see next chapter) provide yet another avenue for the huckster to hype a product. It's an unusual format in that what's written for the ear has to appeal to the eyes. In other words, sound replaces sight so the more noise and music used the better. Burt Wilson applied this theory to his radio spot for *Kidnapped* (1971), a British film version of the Robert Louis Stevenson classic. Wilson didn't see the film nor did he use any dialog from it after being told that no

This scene from Hollywood Boulevard *(New World, 1976) recently turned up in a remake of* Not of This Earth *(1988).*

one would understand the English accents. Instead he culled every battle noise he could find and added some Scottish bagpipes as background to his copy. The results nearly blew the speakers during playback and impressed the company releasing the film.

For five years Wilson wrote radio spots for American International and quickly learned that to AIP there was no such thing as a bad movie, just bad campaigns.

Wilson observed that "AIP looked at a film from a different angle than most major studios." When an independent producer brought a movie in he wanted AIP to take on for distribution, all the top execs took a look at it. For quality? No. Story line? Great acting? No. If any of that existed it was a plus. Their only question was, could they *sell* it. Did it lend itself to an ad campaign that would turn people on. And if it didn't, could anything be changed around to make it saleable ("Confessions of a Hollywood Hitman," by Burt Wilson, *L.A. Reader,* May 4, 1984).

A demonstration of its tenacity with a movie was given by AIP in

God Bless the Bomb (1972), which Wilson was instructed to advertise as an adventure film. It was the story of three prisoners who stole a B-52 loaded with H-bombs which they threatened to use on Fort Knox if the President didn't end the war in Vietnam. The movie didn't make any money as an adventure film so it was withdrawn from release, given a new title — *Wild in the Sky* — and re-released as a comedy. Wilson's new campaign included a drunken version of the Air Force Hymn with an announcer saying, "filmed entirely without the cooperation of the Air Farce . . . er, Force!" That didn't work either, partly because AIP thought they could find an audience by playing the movie near southern Air Force bases. Their target customers didn't take kindly to a film with a homosexual base commander. Then one of the film's players, Georg Stanford Brown, became a regular on *The Rookies* television show. *Wild in the Sky* became *Black Jack*: "He's got the man on the pan and he's gonna fry him good!"

Eight

Spots Before Your Ears

For this chapter I have gone into the vaults and have come up with what I feel are some fine representations of the art form known as the radio spot, both from classic films and some not so classic. The first is from a not-so-classic movie, a spot written by Mr. Burt Wilson who discovered during his five years with AIP that a hint (and it had to be a hint or the Federal Communications Commission would scream) of lesbianism helped sell tickets, even if there was no hint of it in the movie itself, which is definitely the case of *Black Mama, White Mama* (1972; a female version of *The Defiant Ones, 1958*):

"*(Jail noises)* ANNOUNCER: Fate brought them together in the same prison, but their color kept them apart. They endured everything imaginable in a woman's prison and now they were free, a thousand miles from nowhere, locked together by chains, hate, and the erotic desires a woman gets after a thousand nights without a man. They were free . . . but not from each other."

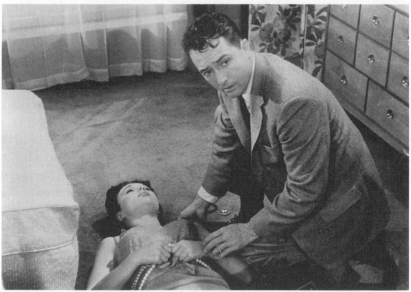

(Top) *Margaret Markov and Pam Grier are chained together in* Black Mama, White Mama *(American International, 1972).* (Bottom) *Robert Clarke discovers a corpse in* Secret File: Hollywood *(Crown International, 1961).*

"SECRET FILE: HOLLYWOOD" (1961)

ANNOUNCER: This is it! . . . A Hollywood scandal magazine exposed. Never before on the screen the unvarnished truth about sensation-seeking headline hunters! . . . What do young girls have to do to get into the movies? . . . How was a famous director framed and blackmailed? . . . Yes, it's all here! . . . *Secret File: Hollywood!* . . . The picture that dares take you behind the studio gates.

"BEDEVILLED" (1955)

ANNOUNCER: In M-G-M's *Bedevilled* we think you'll find a drama that is tops in suspense, in a new and intriguing manner. Imagine that it's nighttime in Paris . . . the Paris you've dreamed about. You walk down the boulevard . . . you hail a cab and step inside . . . then— suddenly—a beautiful girl breaks out of the darkness—runs fearfully across the street and slips into the cab. And there you are together, alone . . . ! It's the start of 24 hours of bizarre adventure in Paris, plunging you into the backstreets, the boulevards and secret hideaways of the world's most fascinating city.

"THE FULLER BRUSH MAN" (1948)

ANNOUNCER: Have you brushed out the bats in your belfry recently? Well, if you haven't, let the screen's funniest man, Red Skelton, do it for you! Yes, sir, Red has just what you need in the way of giggles and guffaws in his starring role as *The Fuller Brush Man,* Columbia Pictures' hilarious new comedy. Red Skelton is the door-to-roar salesman who meets four beautiful women, including m-m-m-m-m-m-m Janet Blair and curvaceous Adele Jergens. Naturally, Red Skelton provides more laughs than a brush has bristles. He's the dizziest Fuller Brush Man who ever rang a doorbell. Fair warning! Any similarity between Red Skelton and your Fuller Brush man is absolutely impossible! When Red Skelton gives a demonstration—the laughter rocks the nation. Wonderful things happen when Red knocks on strange doors . . . because with him every knock's a boost! And every doorbell he rings rings the comedy bell! As *The Fuller Brush Man,* Red Skelton parlays a kitful of brushes into a caseful of murder . . . in parlor, kitchen and clink!

Sultry Diana Dors shows her stuff in this scene from The Unholy Wife *(RKO-Universal, 1957).*

"THE UNHOLY WIFE" (1957)

ANNOUNCER: What sinister passion could drive her to wreak such havoc? How could she be made for love, yet promised to the devil? See this devastating woman . . . half angel . . . half devil . . . who doomed her husband to be half a man. See how *The Unholy Wife* transformed one man's valley paradise into a maelstrom of scandal and murder. See lovely Diana Dors . . . a plaything of flesh and the devil in *The Unholy Wife*. Filmed with lavish artistry . . . in Technicolor.

"THE REDHEAD FROM WYOMING" (1953)

ANNOUNCER: Out of the dust of the ghost towns . . . across the plains of sage and tumbleweed, ride Wyoming's finest once again to tell you the story of *The Redhead from Wyoming* . . . queen of a renegade town, trading in stolen cattle and wanted men . . . ruling her outlaw mavericks, putting a brand on those who dared to play her game. . . . It's the picture that brings you the great Sweetwater Massacre, a gun fighting chill you'll never forget, climaxed in final scenes of tempestuous romance when Cattle Kate turns all woman at last for the only man she finds worth loving. . . . Step up and meet *The Redhead from Wyoming*, the lady who had a weapon for every kind of man, a loaded gun, a ready kiss, and knew how to use them both!

"THE TATTERED DRESS" (1957)

ANNOUNCER: What happened to the woman in the tattered dress? . . . As the men whose reputations were shattered . . . ask the town whose hidden evil was exposed . . . ask the husband who claimed the right to kill under the Unwritten Law! See *The Tattered Dress* . . . a story of a dangerous love—and its aftermath, wanton murder . . . of eight desperate people trapped in its vicious web—and of two who found in their trust of each other the courage to face a hate-ridden town! *The Tattered Dress* . . . overwhelming with sudden suspense . . . raw with the realism of life itself!

"THE LOST WEEKEND" (1945)

ANNOUNCER: Paramount Pictures warns you—get ready for a shock! With uncompromising frankness, pulling no punches, Paramount has filmed the most sensational, talked-about novel of our time! *The Lost Weekend* can now be *seen* with Ray Milland as Don Birnam, a tortured psychopath who staggers down strange forbidden byways for five unforgettable days in search of his soul. It's the story critics and public alike said could never be screened. . . . For the screen shock of your lifetime, you *must* see the year's all-important screen event.

"VOICE IN THE MIRROR" (1958)

ANNOUNCER: Where other pictures only whisper—this drama dares to shout! . . . The brutal and beautiful, the tender and terrifying story of one man's battle against alcoholism . . . and of the girl who crawled back with him every shocking inch of the way! . . . a human experience at once so jolting and devastating . . . so intimate and intense it emerges as motion picture drama second to none! . . . In *Voice in the Mirror* you will see the story of a marriage that existed from night to night, never knowing what tomorrow would bring or what yesterday had done! . . . In *Voice in the Mirror* you will see a woman fight fiercely to save her love . . . never knowing when her husband would be a man again . . . so she could be a wife again.

"THAT NIGHT" (1957)

ANNOUNCER: See the real inside of a theme rarely explored on the screen. See *That Night* of shame. . . . *That Night* of fear. . . . *That Night* of consuming discovery could be *your* night . . . because the screen drama *That Night* reveals the truth about a crisis that could be *your* crisis. If *you* think *you're* happily married, don't miss *That Night*. . . . It's true, factual, unexpurgated. *That Night* . . . as wonderful as tomorrow's sunrise.

"THE PRICE OF FEAR" (1956)

ANNOUNCER: Jolting, jarring drama rips the motion picture screen! . . . See *The Price of Fear!* . . . The suspense-filled story of a half-world that only starts with murder . . . a half-world where every kiss betrays and every bullet has a name on it! . . . Starring Merle Oberon—a woman who tried to kiss away her guilt! . . . Lex Barker—an innocent man trapped between two crimes he didn't commit! . . . Hour by hour the net of terror tightens! Somewhere in the shadows of the city the law and lawless wait in a ring of fear! . . . But for one man— beautifully framed by a desperate woman—there is no escape. . . . If he gives up—he hangs! . . . If he runs—he gets shot down! . . . If he fights back—he drags down with him everything decent he has ever known!

"FORBIDDEN" (1954)

ANNOUNCER: From Chicago, Macao, Hong Kong, the hired killers come . . . watching for the man called Eddie Darrow . . . waiting for the woman whose kiss would mark him for their bullets. . . . From reel to reel the excitement mounts as the motion picture *Forbidden* grips you in its climax of hard bitten action, extreme excitement, nerve snapping suspense . . . and Great *Great* entertainment. . . . When you see *Forbidden* you'll travel to the fabulous island of Macao, last outpost of intrigue. . . . You'll see Tony Curtis in his most dramatic role, as the kind of man who's out of bounds for any kind of woman . . . *Joanne Dru* as the girl he trailed from a penthouse in Chicago to the backstreets of the Orient . . . *Lyle Bettger* as chief of Macao's underworld . . . with blonde *Mamie Van Doren* as the cafe singer on the street of forbidden delights. . . . It's daring . . . it's thrilling . . . it's *Forbidden.*

"HE WALKED BY NIGHT" (1948)

(Sound of footsteps on cement pavement along the waterfront) VOICE: *He Walked by Night. (Fading) He Walked by Night.* AN-NOUNCER: Ladies and Gentlemen, I want you to meet a killer — a cold, brilliant criminal who wrote one of the most violent chapters in the "Homicide" Records of the Los Angeles Police Department! *He Walked by Night* is the *true* inside story of this killer's private war on the city he terrorized . . . the day-by-day account of his murderous career as he followed it to its incredible climax! In *He Walked by Night* you'll see Police Methods never before revealed! A killer's face recreated before your eyes! You'll see a daring chase through deep underground sewers you never knew existed . . . 700 miles of hidden highways stretching beneath the City of Los Angeles! *He Walked by Night* is a Motion Picture that's *true!* It's *stronger than fiction!* See . . . *(Sound of footsteps on cement pavement along the waterfront)* VOICE: *He Walked by Night.* (Fading) *He Walked by Night.*

"T-MEN" (1947)

(Sound of police siren) ANNOUNCER: *T-Men* . . . the screen-shattering story of the Treasury's Tough Guys! *(Burst of machine gun fire)*

ANNOUNCER: *T-Men! (Blast of dynamite)*

ANNOUNCER: *T-Men* dynamites the screen with the raw, savage fury of its telling! See . . . killers plundering, torturing, murdering to build an illicit empire! No one could stop them . . . till a woman's lovely lips opened—and talked too much! Don't miss *Dennis O'Keefe* in . . . *(Police siren)*

ANNOUNCER: . . . *T-Men!* It's tense! *(Blast of dynamite)*

ANNOUNCER: T-Men! It's loaded with dynamite . . . t-e-r-r-i-f-i-c . . . and true! See—*(Machine gun fire)*

ANNOUNCER: *T-Men! T-Men!*

"THE BIG HEAT" (1953)

ANNOUNCER: Four girls are dead! And there's an ex-cop out to avenge them! Yes, the big heat is turned on full blast. . . . *The Big Heat* is the famous *Saturday Evening Post* serial come to life on the screen. *The Big Heat* has all the blood and guts, violence and romance that shocked millions of readers! Vice . . . dice . . . and corruption! They run riot when a tough cop and a soft dame get together! Watch 'em put the big heat on the big town!

"LAND OF FURY" (1954)

ANNOUNCER: For your most exciting, your most thrilling adventure of the year . . . you must see the new J. Arthur Rank motion picture, *Land of Fury!* . . . a story set in the ancient kingdom of the Maori, a forgotten world ruled by strange ritual and savage customs . . . man's last pagan wilderness defying civilization with all its primitive passions . . . actually photographed among the Maori natives of New Zealand. . . . See and thrill to the forbidden secrets of the sacred cave of skulls . . . native war canoes on their errand of death . . . the wild abandon of the dance of love . . . the awesome spectacle of a Maori dance of death . . . see and thrill to a savage world of exotic splendor . . . untamed . . . unconquered!

(Opposite) *Robert Burton and Glenn Ford investigate the suicide of a fellow officer (*The Big Heat, Columbia, 1953).

"EAST OF SUMATRA" (1953)

ANNOUNCER: In the last savage corner of the South Pacific lies the island in whose soil is hidden the wealth all men dream of . . . in its jungles, silent death . . . in its compounds, native girls who have learned the ways of love . . . the compass of high adventure points *East of Sumatra* . . . taking you to a forgotten island of danger and moonlight enchantment . . . bringing you the motion picture story of Duke Mullane . . . the iron men he led . . . the jungle he plundered . . . the native queen who worshipped him and betrayed her own people to earn his love. . . . Here, in the last outpost of spear and poisoned dart, you'll meet *Jeff Chandler* as the man who lived for love of danger, and love of a savage queen . . . *East of Sumatra* . . . to the forbidden interior of an island of thrills!

"TANGANYIKA" (1954)

ANNOUNCER: A white woman, abandoned in the heart of Africa . . . a hunter, merciless as the jungle he fought . . . a white medicine man, God of the jungle tribes . . . a stranger who knew the deadly secret of *Tanganyika* . . . these are the four outcasts who follow crooked trails to a last violent rendezvous in the savage heart of the Congo . . . *Tanganyika* . . . the story of the Englishman Abel McCracken who set himself up in an African kingdom to wage a war of vengeance against the outside world . . . of the brother who tried to save him . . . of the hunter who swore to kill him . . . of the white woman who found that love was the prize, in the most dangerous game of all . . . *Tanganyika* . . . where a madman rules a jungle empire . . . in a dynasty of terror!

"GOLIATH AND THE BARBARIANS" (1959)

ANNOUNCER: When brutal barbarian hordes savagely slashed across the face of the earth, pillaging and ravaging, through it all their leader had one cry . . .

LEADER: Kill them!

ANNOUNCER: Into the bloodshed stepped a fearless leader, young and powerful. *Steve Reeves*, Mister *Hercules* himself in his greatest role.

GOLIATH: I will have my revenge. I swear it. His murderers shall have no peace.

ANNOUNCER: He revenged his father's death by killing 10,000 barbarians. They called him GOLIATH, the greatest of all warriors. Every woman dreamed of his embrace.

WOMAN: I couldn't live without you! We'll go away, my love, just us two. Together.

ANNOUNCER: *Goliath and the Barbarians!* The giant of giants of all great motion picture spectacles.

"ROCK 'N' ROLL HIGH SCHOOL" (1979)

(Title song) ANNOUNCER: *Rock 'n' Roll High School* is an album *and* a movie. Vince Van Patten is *crazy* about P.J. Soles but she wants to live a rock 'n' roll fantasy with her favorite group . . . *The Ramones! (Another song by The Ramones)*

ANNOUNCER: The new principal tries to stop the music but the kids rock 'n' wreck the school! *(Explosion)*

ANNOUNCER: *Rock 'n' Roll High School* . . . the school where the students rule! . . . *Your* school could be next!

"RUNNING WILD" (1955)

ANNOUNCER: They're too young to be careful . . . too tough to be afraid . . . and too smart to get caught. . . . They're today's lost generation . . . running wild! . . . See *Running Wild!* . . . and watch teenage terror explode from the motion picture screen . . . in a story wild and violent as the big city jungles . . . where there's an easy racket for every easy-money hungry punk . . . and a girl to run wild at his side! . . . See teen-age gangs take over the town . . . running a hot-car racket from a secret juke-box dive . . . where an organized juvenile crime ring holds the key to wanton killings! . . . Feel the wild rhythm of Razzle-Dazzle and other great new rock-and-roll dance music! . . . Be jolted by the stark . . . brutal . . . bare-knuckled fury of *Running Wild!*

Members of an all-female gang hang out in this scene from Girls on the Loose.
*Pictured here from left to right: Barbara Bostock, Mara Corday, Joyce Barker,
and Lita Milan (Universal-International, 1958).*

"GIRLS ON THE LOOSE" (1958) *and*
"LIVE FAST, DIE YOUNG" (1958)

ANNOUNCER: Here's that jolting, jarring combination screen
program that hits *you where you live!* ... *Girls on the Loose!* ...
the sensational drama of crime-crazy girls ... love-hungry girls ...
trigger-happy girls ... girls who will stop at nothing ... a story
filled with excitement that cuts like a switch-blade knife! ... Plus
Second Headline Hit! ... *Live Fast, Die Young!* ... the sin-
streaked story of the runaway teenage girls of today's 'beat' generation!
... the motion picture that takes you into the broken homes, the
skid-row bars, the penthouse girl-traps on the one-way highway to
trouble!

"FRANCIS JOINS THE WACS" (1954)

ANNOUNCER: There ought to be a National Award for fun! . . . to *Francis,* the talking Mule . . . for the funniest, the *cra*—ziest, the most hilarious motion picture since Hollywood began . . . to *Donald O'Connor* for the greatest comedy of his brilliant career . . . to *Francis Joins the Wacs* . . . the motion picture that's funnier than people. . . . Yes, that screwy Looie and his four-legged pal are back again in the ladies' army now and it's the funniest mistake since the mule learned to talk. Redheads to the right of 'em, blondes to the left of 'em. With *Donald* as the only man living in the women's barracks . . . and, man, what a living! . . . and the Wacs are simply wacky over *Francis!*

"THE KETTLES ON OLD MACDONALD'S FARM" (1957)

ANNOUNCER: Get an acre of laughs . . . a barn-full of fun with the newest . . . wildest . . . happiest adventures of that wonderful Kettle family! . . . Yes, there's a bumper crop of Kettle kids romping in the pasture . . . a blessed event on the way . . . a hungry grizzly bear stalking their trail . . . and a pair of young lovers hiding in the barn! *The Kettles on Old MacDonald's Farm* is fun galore! . . . every giggle . . . every guffaw . . . every roar a riot of laughter! . . . See America's fun-famed family in their craziest hit by a country mile!

"SLIM CARTER" (1957)

ANNOUNCER: Here's the most hilarious, heart-warming movie since *The Private War of Major Benson* ––– *Slim Carter!* ––– the wild and wonderful adventures of a made-in-Hollywood hero and the half-pint orphan who cut him down to size! . . . Starring Jock Mahoney as Slim . . . who had a hundred million fans and not one friend to his name! . . . Julie Adams . . . who built him into a legend—and fell in love with the man! . . . and Tim Hovey as Shorty—who takes off with your heart when he takes on the West's biggest hero! . . . Hear Jock sing some swell new songs! . . . Watch tiny, terrific Tim Hovey give the West that Major Benson treatment! . . . Yes, folks— if you're four or a hundred and forty you'll love Slim and Shorty!

Two of Universal-International's bread-and-butter movies. (Top) *Marjorie Main and Percy Kilbride in* The Kettles on Old MacDonald's Farm *(1957).* (Bottom) *Donald O'Connor and Francis, the Talking Mule, from* Francis Goes to the Races *(1951).*

"THE NIGHT WALKER" (1964)

ANNOUNCER: This is the voice of a woman dreaming about her lover.

WOMAN'S VOICE: Oh, please darling, hold me close. I love you so much.

ANNOUNCER: And this . . . a woman having a nightmare.

WOMAN'S VOICE: Let me out. Aaaaaaaaahhhhhhhhh!

ANNOUNCER: What are dreams? What do they mean? When you dream you wander into another world where everything is strange and terrifying. . . . When you dream you too become a . . . *Night Walker*. *The Night Walker* brings Robert Taylor and Barbara Stanwyck together again in this film shocker of the year.

STANWYCK: Yes, I *do* have a lover.

TAYLOR: Tell me his name!

STANWYCK: I wish to God I could but he's only a dream.

ANNOUNCER: And now . . . a warning from producer William Castle.

CASTLE: Our new picture, *The Night Walker*, may force you to dream of things you're ashamed to admit. If you can't stand your own dreams . . . don't see *The Night Walker*.

"THE UNINVITED" (1944)

(*Ghostly sobbing*)   ANNOUNCER: Hear that! It's the voice of *The Uninvited* . . . in a house of horror . . . where the living are clutched by icy terror of the restless dead.

CRISP: When you were a little child, after her death, the evils of this house reached out for you. I took you away then. If I could only take you now. Stella go! Go!

RUSSELL: Grandfather! (*Screams*)

ANNOUNCER: *The Uninvited!* Paramount's gripping picturization of Dorothy Macardle's novel of the supernatural . . . starring Ray Milland, Ruth Hussey, Donald Crisp . . . with Cornelia Otis Skinner and lovely Gail Russell. (*Ghostly sobbing again*)

ANNOUNCER: There are no such things as ghosts, you say? Then *you're* one of those who dare to see . . . *The Uninvited!*

"BLACK SUNDAY" (1960)

(*Dripping sound*) ANNOUNCER: The sound you hear is dripping blood. This is the start of *Black Sunday*. (*Thunder clap*)

ANNOUNCER: *Black Sunday* comes but once every hundred years. On that day the undead demons of hell rise to unleash an orgy of evil on the world. American International presents *Black Sunday* . . . the most frightening motion picture you have ever seen. (*Thunder clap*)

ANNOUNCER: She was murdered 500 years ago . . . there in the barren waste that was her cemetery they nailed the mask of Satan to her face. (*Scream . . . the sound of hammering*)

ANNOUNCER: Not since Dracula stalked the earth has there been such an unspeakable day and night as . . . *Black Sunday!*

"THE HAUNTED STRANGLER" (1958)

(*Sound of heavy breathing*) ANNOUNCER: Hear that sound? Frightening, isn't it? It's *The Haunted Strangler* . . . and here to tell you about him is *Boris Karloff*.

KARLOFF: Hell—it's funny. *The Haunted Strangler* . . . he goes around at night . . . and he comes quietly up behind you . . . and then. . . . Well (*chuckles*). . . . You can imagine what happens. But why imagine. See *The Haunted Strangler!* And by the way on the same movie program there's a second masterpiece of horror . . . *Fiend Without a Face.* . . . It's about weird little creatures made by atomic energy . . . loathsome things that kill you by eating your brains!

ANNOUNCER: Don't miss *Karloff*, King of the Monsters, in *The Haunted Strangler* plus *Fiend Without a Face.* . . . Both terrifying hits from M-G-M.

"KISS ME KATE" (1953)

ANNOUNCER: You've never really seen 3-D until you've seen M-G-M's wonderful new musical color spectacle—*Kiss Me Kate!* Because M-G-M took this great Samuel and Bella Spewack Broadway hit and *filmed it especially for 3-D*. The result . . . pictures so sharp . . . so clear . . . so perfectly third-dimensional that you will feel as though the players were actually on the stage . . . singing and dancing before you!

Donald O'Connor, Debbie Reynolds, King Donovan, Gene Kelly, and Jean Hagen, from Singin' in the Rain. *(M-G-M, 1952.)*

"HEY! LET'S TWIST!" (1961)

ANNOUNCER: Teenagers in blue jeans . . . high society blueblood . . . ivy-leaguers . . . Junior leaguers . . . and Little leaguers. . . . Everyone. . . . Everywhere is doing the *TWIST!* So, come on . . . *Hey! Let's Twist!* The one great movie about *the* sensation that's sweeping the nation . . . with the stars and music that started it . . . *Joey Dee and The Starliters, Jo-Ann Campbell, Teddy Randazzo and The Peppermint Loungers!* . . . Yes, Paramount Pictures presents the only *authentic* motion picture about the magnificent madness that's twisting across the world into the hearts of young and old!

"SINGIN' IN THE RAIN" (1952)

ANNOUNCER: Okay, fellows, and gals . . . this is it! You sopranos . . . stand over there . . . and you, altos, you stand next to them. . . . Now the tenors here . . . and the baritones there. . . . And the basses . . . well, stay right where you are! When I say "go" step right out singin' . . . *Singin' in the Rain*. . . . Yessir, it's a glorious feeling singin' in the rain and it's the title of another glorious M-G-M musical!. . . You'll be happy again when you see *Gene Kelly, Donald O'Connor* and that wonderful "aba daba" girl *Debbie Reynolds* in the rainbow Technicolor hit *Singin' in the Rain!*

"GUNSMOKE" (1953)

ANNOUNCER: When the deadliest hired gun in the West was turned on the land of the lawless—the spoiler rule of Montana's land-locked mountain empire was smashed! That is the exciting story of *Gunsmoke*—the dramatic motion picture based on the first great drive to the Yellowstone. *Gunsmoke*—starring Audie Murphy as the gun-slinger whose gun was bought by a woman's kisses—Susan Cabot as the girl who found love on the vengeance trail across 1000 treacherous miles—Paul Kelly as the man too tough to be scared, too old to run— and Charles Drake as the trigger-man who signed on to wipe out his pal! *Gunsmoke*—takes you on the spectacular trek through plunging moun-tain death and renegade ambush—when one man drove a maddened herd and mutinous men through raging scrub-fire and over icy peaks to the richest range on the frontier . . . a story of vengeance, of six-gun rule—and of love born in peril.

"THE NAKED DAWN" (1955)

ANNOUNCER: He was a saint, this stranger who rode out of the naked dawn . . . and he was a rogue . . . a generous, lusty, likeable rogue . . . who lived for today and let the devil take care of tomorrow . . . and for those he befriended or betrayed . . . life was never the same

... you'll meet him ... know him ... in *The Naked Dawn* ... a penetrating drama of passion and violence ... an exciting motion picture story of a bandit who almost destroys the loves and lives of a young farmer and his beautiful wife ... to one he brought the excitement of high adventure ... and the corroding sickness of greed ... to the other ... hungry for love ... he brought the hope of freedom ... of escape ... but most of all ... to her ... he was a man.... See *The Naked Dawn* ... emotions as elemental ... as powerful as life itself!

"RAW EDGE" (1956)

ANNOUNCER: On the wild Oregon frontier in 1852 ... violent men made their own law ... and women lived on the raw edge of jeopardy ... a savage land where a woman's love belonged to the first man who claimed it—the spoils of the strongest, the boldest, or the fastest with a gun!... *Raw Edge* ... starring Rory Calhoun, the stranger who came in peace but stayed for vengeance!... Yvonne de Carlo, dangerous as only a woman can be in a land of lawless men! ... filled with fury of the untamed frontier and one man's daring fight for justice ... against the desperate and the damned—and the ruthless empire they forged out of a lust for power!

"FORBIDDEN PLANET" (1956)

ANNOUNCER: M-G-M takes you on a fabulous adventure—far beyond the farthest star!... *Forbidden Planet* ... far and away the most provocative and unusual film you've ever seen! You'll fly in a giant space ship of 2200 A.D. to the planet Altair-4 in outer space ... the *Forbidden Planet!* You'll discover an exciting, undreamed of world of green skies, two moons and wonderful mechanical marvels. Meet a blonde beauty living in fantastic luxury! Marvel at the fascinating mechanical genius of Robby the Robot! And over everything on this strange *Forbidden Planet* hovers an unknown, unnamed invisible menace that suddenly attacks the Earth-men in a spectacular war of the future! And it's all climaxed by the explosion of the planet into a fiery inferno! Here is an

amazing motion picture . . . M-G-M's *Forbidden Planet*—the thrilling story of Man's leap to the stars . . . in wondrous Color and CinemaScope!

"THE TIME MACHINE" (1960)

MAN: Can you face the future? (*Sound of an explosion*)

ANNOUNCER: Can you exist in a world of atomic war? (*High frequency sound*)

MAN: Can you travel with the speed of sound?

ANNOUNCER: Move through the 4th Dimension?

MAN: Crash the barriers of space and time into another age? (*Sonic boom wipes frequency tone*)

ANNOUNCER: Metro-Goldwyn-Mayer presents—

MAN: George Pal's production of H.G. Wells' astounding tale—

ANNOUNCER: *The Time Machine!*

MAN: Starring Rod Taylor, Alan Young, Yvette Mimieux. (*Sound of rocket streaking past*)

ANNOUNCER: *The Time Machine!*

MAN: Takes you on a rocketing flight into unknown worlds. . . .

ANNOUNCER: Eight hundred thousand years into the future! (*Sound of avalanche*)

MAN: You'll feel *terror* in a world that sinks beneath your feet! (*Monster growl*)

ANNOUNCER: You'll know terror in the night as monsters prowl the dark!

MAN: You'll see terror in the depths as man-eating creatures from the earth's core threaten all humanity!

ANNOUNCER: *The Time Machine!*

MAN: The picture that smashes the time barrier!

ANNOUNCER: That shows you the future before it happens!

MAN: See—on the giant screen in blazing color—

ANNOUNCER: *The Time Machine!*

(Opposite) *Jack Kelly, Warren Stevens, Leslie Nielsen, Walter Pidgeon and Robbie the Robot from* Forbidden Planet *(M-G-M, 1956).*

Rod Taylor battles the Morlocks in The Time Machine *(M-G-M, 1960).*

"THE MAD MAGICIAN" (1954)

ANNOUNCER: Mad lover!... Mad killer!... Mad Magician!... See Vincent Price as *The Mad Magician* ... doing tricks of magic and murder never before seen on any stage or screen!... Girls' heads sawed off!... Men burned alive!... See how Vincent Price combines magic ... and murder!

"FOXFIRE" (1955)

ANNOUNCER: Jane's got Jeff!... Yes, Jane Russell's got Jeff Chandler ... and how! ... in *Foxfire*.... The impassioned motion picture story of an impatient love ... flaming to daring life from the exciting pages of Anya Seton's best-selling novel ... starring the screen's most combustible lovers ... Jane Russell and Jeff Chandler ... lost in each other's arms ... aroused by restless longings ... aflame with fury defying society's walls that should keep them worlds apart ... they're reckless in their ecstacy ... as their great love draws them irresistibly together.... Yes, Jane's got Jeff alright ... and wait 'till you see how she *holds* him!

"THE RESTLESS YEARS" (1958)

ANNOUNCER: What happens when a girl first feels a woman's need? ... and a boy first faces a man's desire?... *The Restless Years* tells the whole dramatic story ... electrifyingly exposes the morals, the mistakes, the shame, the scandal of a town with a "dirty mind" ... when ugly rumors ... evil gossip ... can make a decent girl a target for the teen-age pack ... and turn a tender young romance into a nightmare of disgrace.... *The Restless Years* ... that shape all our lives ... have now been shaped into a tremendous motion picture ... moving, shocking ... yet tender and unforgettably romantic.

"FOUR GIRLS IN TOWN" (1957)

ANNOUNCER: Here's the kind of gay love adventure every girl lives in her dreams!... See *Four Girls in Town* ... the scintillating story of

four shapely beauties from the four corners of the earth . . . who found
in glamorous Hollywood a career in their grasp . . . men on their minds
. . . and the kind of excitement every woman wants! . . . living the kind
of story that could happen only in the town where stars are born . . .
where happiness and heartbreak go hand in hand . . . where the lovely
and the lonely tell a grand—and wonderful story!. . . Meet the small-
town girl with big-town ideas . . . the girl who ran away from the man
she couldn't live without . . . the girl who had one man in her memories,
another in her arms! . . . and the girl with eyes only for men, money and
matrimony. . . . They're simply wonderful!

In *The Maltese Falcon* (1941) Humphrey Bogart listened to Elisha
Cook mouth a string of empty threats then noted, "The cheaper the
crook the gaudier the patter." I feel that line applies, with perhaps a
slight alteration, to the folks who cooked up the array of alliterations,
the plethora of expletives, and the generous dose of vulgarity that you've
been reading.

There have been times, it should be noted, when the show is more
than a match for the hawker. When *King Kong* opened in March of 1933,
the national magazine ads claimed it was "destined to startle the world!"
The exhibitors were told the picture was full of enough dramatic
dynamite to blast show business from the grip of lethargy. Which it did.
The picture opened at the Radio City Music Hall and the New Roxy,
New York's two largest theatres, the first picture to play both houses
simultaneously. Audiences were stunned. In its first four days it set a
world attendance record. Two decades later, in a one-minute radio
spot, one campaign man referred to *Kong* as "the biggest gorilla picture
ever made!" Back in '33 it commanded more respect. Back in '33 a one-
minute radio spot wasn't enough.

One month before the picture hit New York, "Hollywood on the
Air" presented a program which was, in essence, an extended radio
spot. Here's how it began—and then some excerpts are provided from
throughout the roughly 15-minute program.

FANFARE: Trumpets.

ANNOUNCER: Hollywood-on-the-Air.

FANFARE: Trumpets—segue into theme.

ANNOUNCER: Hollywood-on-the-Air, coming to you from our
Radio Pictures Studio in Hollywood, California. When the last page is
torn from the calendar this year, motion picture history will have

a new chapter—a chapter dedicated to the courage and vision of two men who dared to make come true the greatest dream Hollywood has ever known. These men are Merian C. Cooper and Ernest B. Schoedsack—and the dream fulfilled is their mighty Radio Production, *King Kong*. This, truly, is the film news event of 1933! Two years of actual camera work, in addition to many years of thought and planning, have been injected into this mammoth film, so you may, for two short hours, soon be entertained and enthralled in your favorite theatre. Tonight, over this network reaching from ocean to ocean and making it possible to enter millions of homes, *King Kong*, the giant jungle beast—

SOUND: KING KONG ROAR.

ANNOUNCER: That invaded civilization in search of a flaming-haired girl, will stalk across your threshold—to amaze you—to startle you—to entertain you!

SOUND: KING KONG ROAR.

ORCHESTRA: *(Pick up immediately after roar)* "Young and Healthy."

ANNOUNCER: For his distinctive achievement in coproducing and codirecting *King Kong* with Ernest B. Schoedsack, Merian C. Cooper has been rewarded. This reward has been his appointment to the position of executive vice-president in charge of all production for Radio Pictures. Congratulations, Merian C. Cooper and Ernest B. Schoedsack. To you, Hollywood-on-the-Air presents a musical salute.

ORCHESTRA: SALUTE.

. . .

RAY FERNSTROM: Good evening, lovers of adventure and motion pictures—everywhere. Once again, we're standing by our cameras. Once again, the hunt for news is under way. This time—the news is *King Kong*. What is *King Kong*? How did it begin? Who is this man Merian C. Cooper? And why is *King Kong* news? King Kong is a fifty-foot ape with the bark of thunder in his lungs and the strength of many giants in his hands. A man-made Robot of a forgotten land,—Skull Island—King Kong dominates the most thrilling and fantastic adventure film ever conceived. Merian C. Cooper and Ernest B. Schoedsack, who together gave the world its most memorable adventure films— *Grass* and *Chang*— now produce the headline picture of 1933—*King Kong*. The remote corners of the globe; the densest jungles bear the wandering foot-prints of Cooper and Schoedsack, whose motto has always been: "If it exists, it can be photographed." Why is *King Kong* news? Because it marks the turning point in screen entertainment. With twelve reels of exciting celluloid, it sets a new goal in the amusement world. What was the origin of *King Kong*? How did it come into being? We'll start at the beginning.

. . .

REPORTER: If I had been in all the strange places you've been, Mr. Cooper—fought as many wars—and that sort of thing,—I'd retire. Buy a chicken ranch, you know, the kind you read about in the Chamber of Commerce ads—and settle down.

COOPER: I've got it! I've got it!

REPORTER: What? A chicken ranch?

COOPER: No—an idea.

REPORTER: Good. What is it?

MERIAN C. COOPER: . . . don't repeat [this] to a soul until I get the picture under way.

REPORTER: It's a promise.

COOPER: I was just thinking. Persia, where Schoedsack and I made *Grass*; Siam, where we made *Chang*, and all the other colorful spots where we have made films—Borneo, Sumatra and the Archepelago—no longer is there any mystery or hidden adventure in those places. Although there are a few spots left to explore, I can't give up the idea of making adventure films. And, this very obstacle—or the music—has made me dream again. And that dream is: If I had it in my power to plot the greatest adventure of a life-time, one I could actually participate in, what would it be?

REPORTER: Well, you'll have to answer your own riddles.

COOPER: It would be this. Halfway around the world, somewhere in the Malay waters, there would be an unexplored land known as Skull Island. On this Island would dwell a tribe of strange savages, but not half so queer as their god, whom they worship—a frightful god known to them as King Kong—a towering beast, fifty-feet in height—who would have the power to crush a human being in the palm of his hand. To capture that animal and to bring him back to Broadway, New York, to my way of thinking, would be swell adventure. I don't know what the details of the story would be—I only know that in the story I would have a crazy motion picture producer go in search of this monster. He would take with him a motion picture company which would include only one girl. This powerful beast, King Kong, who never in all his life had gazed on

a beautiful thing, would be strangely attracted to this pretty, white girl —
attracted to her, perhaps, as he might be to some frail but beautiful
flower. In some manner I would bring this beast back to New York —
and then the monster — thinking of this beautiful, human toy — but I'm
telling too much of the story.

REPORTER: I'm sorry I promised not to print this, Mr. Cooper. This
would make a great news yarn. How about giving me permission to print it?

COOPER: I should say not. But, I'll tell you what I will do — as soon as King Kong becomes a reality and is walking around the RKO Lot, ready for his debut in motion pictures, I'll let you break the story.

. . . REPORTER: That's okay with me. Give brother Kong my regards.

SOUND: TUG-BOAT WHISTLES; FERRY-BOAT CHUGGING SWISHING OF WATER.

RAY FERNSTROM: Behind us—the gray silhouette of needle-like buildings. Before us—The Narrows—many oceans—and somewhere far ahead lies romance, adventure, thrills amid a band of prehistoric creatures. A ship rides at anchor by the pier. It is the Venture, manned by strange men and bound on a strange journey. In the dusk of a foggy dawn, the crew is going onboard. There is Carl Denham, the film producer and soldier of fortune, portrayed by Robert Armstrong. He is accompanied by Ann Darrow, played by Fay Wray, whom he found on the sidewalks of New York. She is young, pretty—her eyes eager for the great experience that lies beyond the horizon. There goes Driscoll, the first mate, enacted by Bruce Cabot . . . and there's old Englehorn, the skipper of the craft, played by Frank Reicher.

SOUND: GANGPLANK NOISE: RATTLE OF CHAINS; TUG-BOAT WHISTLE.

. . .

DRISCOLL: Mr. Denham, I'm going to do some butting-in.

DENHAM: What's your trouble, Driscoll?

DRISCOLL: When do we find out where we're going?

DENHAM: Pretty soon now.

DRISCOLL: Are you going to tell us what happens when we get there?

DENHAM: How can I? I'm not a fortune-teller.

DRISCOLL: But hang it, you must have some idea what you're after.

DENHAM: Going soft on me, Jack?

DRISCOLL: You know I'm not for myself—But Ann—

DENHAM: Oh you've gone soft on her? I've got enough on my hands without a love-affair to complicate things. Better cut it out, Jack.

DRISCOLL: (SUDDENLY) Love-affair! You think I'm going to fall for any dame!

DENHAM: (MUSING) It never fails. Some big hard-boiled egg goes goofy over a pretty face, and bingo! he cracks up and gets sappy.

DRISCOLL: (ANGRY) Who's getting sappy? I haven't run out on you, have I?

DENHAM: Nope. You're a good tough guy, Jack. But if beauty gets you—(STOPS, THEN LAUGHS A LITTLE) Why, I'm going right into a theme song!

DRISCOLL: (SULKY) What are you talking about?

DENHAM: It's the idea for my picture. The Beast was a tough guy, Jack. He could lick the world. But when he saw beauty, she got him. He went soft, he forgot his wisdom, and the little fellers licked him. Think it over, Jack.

. . .

RAY FERNSTROM: Through the lowering fog can faintly be discerned the fantastic, grotesque features of the tremendous skull, fashioned by nature from a towering mountain.

SOUND: BABBLE OF UNINTELLIGIBLE VOICES; WEIRD CHANT-ING; SOUND OF TOM-TOMS AND THE ROAR OF KING KONG. TOM-TOMS BEAT THROUGHOUT FOLLOWING SPEECH:

RAY FERNSTROM: From the shore comes the weird chant of many babbling voices and the rhythmic monotone of tom-toms. The fog lowers and through the jungle growth can be seen a thousand black warriors, participating in a weird, native ceremony.

SOUND: BABBLING VOICES OF BLACKS. THE SOUND OF TOM-TOMS CONTINUES THROUGHOUT FOLLOWING SPEECH.

RAY FERNSTROM: The half-naked Blacks, thousands of them, are forming in a giant circle about a young native girl, clothed in beads and resplendent raiment. It is a weird ceremony indeed. Ani saba Kong!—meaning in the tribal language—"She is the bride of Kong." The natives are now paying homage in music to the girl captive.

ORCHESTRA: JUNGLE CHANT.

RAY FERNSTROM: Adventure, death, romance, and thrills have gone hand in hand. Months have flown by. And the good ship, Venture, has sailed away with her guarded secret—a secret that will amaze you, when you see *King Kong*.

. . .

COOPER: Ladies and gentlemen: . . . Willis O'Brien, Hollywood's most noted technical expert, is here in the studio with us. He is a scholar on the subject of anthropology and has spent more than twenty years in the study of prehistoric life. I want you to meet this man who has labored for more than two years in making *King Kong* become a reality. Mr. O'Brien:

WILLIS O'BRIEN: Thank you, Mr. Cooper. I left the projection room here at the studio a few minutes ago where I saw our completed handiwork—*King Kong*. In the near future, it will be showing in your city. It will take you about two hours to see it. Two hours! Into that finished product of two hours, we have crammed many years of hard work in an effort to bring you something entirely new—the conflict of prehistoric creatures with modern man and civilization. Speaking for myself, *King Kong* represents the goal of more than twenty years. For that long a time—and that is a long time in motion pictures—I have delved into by-gone periods, studied the life of animals long before the descent of man—preparing myself for the day when someone would dare to reproduce on the screen the giant beasts that once ruled the world. Without knowing it, I was waiting for *King Kong*. That is the picture for which I have studied twenty years. I feel it has been worth the long years of research. And I hope you, too, will feel the same way after seeing *King Kong*. Thank you.

Nine

Epilogue: The Good Old Days

My father spoke wistfully of the days when he'd go to the movies and for one dime see a newsreel, a cliffhanger, a cartoon, and a feature. I had a taste of that bargain, only by the time I came along a child's ticket cost a quarter and the only places in town running newsreels were the drive-ins. But I never really understood what going to the movies meant until one afternoon when I was sitting in the balcony of a theater called the Globe in downtown Los Angeles.

I suspect the Globe was built in the late 1920s. Like the surrounding area it had fallen on hard times, its luster buried beneath years of dust and soil. The air smelled of sweat and old cigarettes, like one of those side street bars that cater to depression. I was treating the place disrespectfully by resting my feet on the seat in front of me when during intermission my attention was drawn to a box seat at the side of the theater. It was something I would have expected to find if I'd gone to the ballet or the opera, a highly unlikely event to be sure, but I knew of such things. I'd seen them in the movies.

At the bottom of the screen was an orchestra pit, or what had once been an orchestra pit. And for the first time I noticed the elaborate murals and all of the little doodads carved in the walls and I was flabbergasted by what I saw. It may have been gaudy but it was a work of art. It struck me (because I'm a pretty sharp guy) that in its heyday, the Globe must have been quite a place.

In the back of my mind, during my research when I read about all of the elaborate promotional stunts various exhibitors pulled, I always saw them happening at the Globe. Not the Globe I saw that afternoon, but the one I imagined it had once been. Because the Globe *was* ballyhoo, designed to awe. And it wasn't even the best of the bunch. But I'll bet when it was fresh its opulence could make someone forget their troubles for an hour or two and help prep them for the fantasy world they were about to see on the screen. All of the stunts described in this book had that same goal in mind. Maybe they were vulgar but who cared, if they worked. Today a movie is on its own. All of the primers are gone. They stopped making cliffhangers in the mid-1950s, cartoons are on television, the ballyhoo boys have all gone home, and the theaters have all but returned to the tiny converted stores where movies first began. And if I sound like an old fart longing for "the good old days" it's because I am. The funny part is I wasn't really around for "the good old days." Some of the theaters I regularly attended were only slightly bigger than the multiplex crackerboxes that have become the theaters of the 1980s. But there were plenty of them that were a lot better too. Even the worst of them though *looked* like theaters. Now they look like fast food places.

Some people, I suppose, would say we're too sophisticated for all that Barnum and Bailey hoopla. Maybe so. But I still miss it.

Filmography of
Works Mentioned in Text

The Amazing Transparent Man (1959) B&W 58 minutes
Starring Marguerite Chapman, Douglas Kennedy, James Griffith, Ivan Triesault, Red Morgan, Cormel Daniel, Edward Erwin, Jonathan Ledford, Norman Smitch, Patrick Cranshaw, Kevin Kelly, Dennis Adams, and Stacy Morgan.
Directed by Edgar Ulmer, Produced by Lester Guthrie, Screenplay by Jack Lewis, Photographed by Meredith M. Nicholson, Special Effects by Robert George, Music by Darrell Calker.
An American International Release.

The Angry Red Planet (1960) Color/Cinemagic 93 minutes
Starring Gerald Mohr, Nora Hayden, Les Tremayne, Jack Kruschen, Paul Hahn, J. Edward McKinley, Tom Daly, Edward Innes, Gordon Barnes, Jack Haddock, Don Lamond, Brandy Bryan, Joan Fitzpatrick, Duke Morton, William Remick, Fred Ross, and David De Haven.
Directed by Ib Melchior, Produced by Sid Pink and Norman Maurer, Screenplay by Ib Melchior and Sid Pink from a story by Sid Pink, Photographed

by Stanley Cortez, Special Effects by Herman Townsley, Music by Paul Dunlap.

An American International Release.

The Animal World (1956) Color 86 minutes

Narration by Theodore Von Eltz and John Storm.

Directed, Produced and Screenplay by Irwin Allen, Special Effects by Ray Harryhausen and Willis O'Brien, Music by Paul Sawtell.

Warner Brothers.

The Bat (1959) B&W 80 minutes

Starring Vincent Price, Agnes Moorehead, Gavin Gordon, John Sutton, Lenita Lane, Elaine Edwards, Darla Hood, John Bryant, Harvey Stephens, Mike Steele, Riza Royce, Robert B. Williams.

Directed and Screenplay by Crane Wilbur from the play by Mary Roberts Rinehart and Avery Hopwood, Produced by C.J. Tevlin, Art Direction by David Milton, Music by Louis Forbes.

Allied Artists.

The Beast of Hollow Mountain (1956) Color/Regiscope/CinemaScope 81 minutes

Starring Guy Madison, Patricia Medina, Eduardo Noriega, Carlos Rivas, Mario Navarro, Garcia Pena, Julio Villareal, Lupe Carriles, Manuel Arvide, Margarito Luna, Roberto Contreas, Lobo Negro.

Directed by Edward Nassour and Ismael Rodriguez, Produced by Edward and William Nassour, Screenplay by Robert Hill, Ismael Rodriguez and Carlos Orellana from a story by Willis O'Brien, Photographed by Jorge Stahol, Jr., Art Direction by Jack De Witt, Special Effects by Jack Rabin and Louis De Witt, Music by Raul Lavista.

A United Artists Release.

Berserk (1967) Color 96 minutes

Starring Joan Crawford, Ty Hardin, Diana Dors, Michael Gough, Judy Geeson, Robert Hardy, Geoffrey Keen, Sydney Tafler, George Claydon, Philip Madoc, Ambrosine Phillpotts, Thomas Cimarro, Peter Burton, Golda Casimir, Ted Lune, Milton Reid, Marianne Stone, Miki Iveria, Howard Goorney, Reginald Marsh, Bryan Pringle.

Directed by Jim O'Connolly, Produced by Herman Cohen, Screenplay by Aben Kandel and Herman Cohen Art Direction by Maurice Pelling, Music by Patrick John Scott.

Warner Brothers.

The Big Heat (1953) B&W 90 minutes

Starring Glenn Ford, Gloria Grahame, Jocelyn Brando, Alexander Scourby, Lee Marvin, Jeanette Nolan, Peter Whitney, Willis Bouchey, Robert Burton, Adam Williams, Howard Wendell, Cris Alcaide, Michael Granger, Dorothy Green, Carolyn Jones, Ric Roman, Dan Seymour, and Edith Evanson.

Directed by Fritz Lang, Produced by Robert Arthur, Screenplay by

Sydney Boehm based on the *Saturday Evening Post* serial by William P. McGivern, Photographed by Charles Lang, Art Direction by Robert Peterson, Musical Direction by Mischa Bakaleinikoff.

The Blood Spattered Bride (1969) Color 83 minutes
Starring Simon Andrew, Maribel Martin, Dean Selmier, and Alexandra Bastedo.
Directed and Screenplay by Vincent Aranda, Produced by Antonio Perez Olea.
Europix.

The Boy and the Pirates (1960) Color/Perceptovision 82 minutes
Starring Charles Herbert, Susan Gordon, Murvyn Vye, Paul Guilfoyle, Joseph Turkel, Archie Duncan, Than Wyenn, Al Cavens, Mickey Finn, Morgan Jones, and Timothy Carey.
Directed, Produced, and Special Effects by Bert Ira Gordon, Screenplay by Lillie Hayward and Jerry Sackeim, Photographed by Ernest Haller, Art Direction by Edward L. Iiou, Music by Albert Glasser.
A United Artists Release.

Brides of Blood (1962) Color 95 minutes
Starring John Ashley, Beverly Hills, and Kent Taylor.
Directed by Eddie Romero and Gerrardo de Leon, Produced by Eddie Romero.
Hemisphere.

Burn Witch, Burn (1962) B&W 90 minutes
Starring Janet Blair, Peter Wyngarde, Margaret Johnston, Anthony Nicholls, Colin Gordon, Kathleen Byron, Reginald Beckwith, Jessica Dunning, Norman Bird, Judith Stott, and Bill Mitchell.
Directed by Sidney Hayers, Produced by Albert Fennell, Screenplay by Richard Matheson and Charles Beaumont from the novel "Conjure Wife" by Fritz Lieber, Photographed by Reginald Wyer, Art Direction by Jack Shampan, Music by Peter Lamont.
American International.

Bwana Devil (1953) Color/3-D 79 minutes
Starring Robert Stack, Barbara Britton, Nifel Bruce, and Paul McVey.
Directed, Produced, and Screenplay by Arch Oboler.
A United Artists Release.

Cannibal Girls (1973) Color 84 minutes
Starring Eugene Levy, Andrea Martin, Ronald Ulrich, Randall Carpenter, Bonnie Neison, Mira Pawluk, Bob McHeady, Alan Gordon, Allan Price, Earl Pomerantz, and May Jarvis.
Directed by Ivan Reitman, Produced by Daniel Goldberg, Screenplay by Robert Sandler, Special Effects by Richard Whyte and Michael Lotosky, Music by Doug Riley.
An American International Release.

Carousel (1956) Color/CinemaScope 55 128 minutes
 Starring Gordon MacRae, Shirley Jones, Cameron Mitchell, Barbara Ruick, and Robert Rounseville.
 Directed by Henry Kind, Produced by Henry Ephron, Screenplay by Phoebe and Henry Ephron based on "Liliom" by Ferenc Molnar, Lyrics by Oscar Hammerstein II, Music by Richard Rodgers.
 20th Century–Fox.

Cat-Women of the Moon (1953) B&W/3-D 64 minutes
 Starring Sonny Tufts, Victor Jory, Marie Windsor, Bill Phipps, Douglas Fowley, Carol Brewster, Suzanne Alexander, Susan Morrow, Judy Walsh, Betty Allen, Ellye Marshall, and Roxann Delman.
 Directed by Arthur Hilton, Produced by Al Zimbalist and Jack Rabin, Screenplay by Roy Hamilton, Photographed by William Whitely, Art Direction by William Glasgow, Special Effects by Jack Rabin, Music by Elmer Bernstein.
 An Astor Release.

Chamber of Horrors (1966) Color 99 minutes
 Starring Cesare Danova, Wilfrid Hyde-White, Laura Devon, Patrice Wymore, Suzy Parker, Tun Tun, Philip Bourneuf, Jeanette Nolan, Marie Windsor, Patrick O'Neal, Wayne Rogers, Vinton Hayworth, Richard O'Brien, Inger Stratton, Berry Kroeger, Charles Seel, and Ayllene Gibbons.
 Directed and Produced by Hy Averback, Screenplay by Stephen Kanel from a story by Ray Russell and Stephen Kanel, Photographed by Richard Kline, Art Direction by Art Loel, Music by William Lava.
 Warner Brothers.

The Charge at Feather River (1953) Color/3-D 96 minutes
 Starring Gur Madison, Frank Lovejoy, Helen Westcott, Vera Miles, Dick Wesson, Onslow Stevens, and Steve Brodie. Directed by Gordon Douglas, Produced by David Weisbart, Screenplay by James R. Webb, Music by Max Steiner.
 Warner Brothers.

Clash of the Titans (1981) Color/Dynamation 118 minutes
 Starring Harry Hamlin, Judi Bowker, Burgess Meredith, Sean Phillips, Maggie Smith, Claire Bloom, Ursula Andress, Laurence Olivier.
 Directed by Desmond Davis, Produced by Ray Harryhausen and Charles H. Schneer, Screenplay by Beverly Cross, Special Effects by Ray Harryhausen and Jim Danforth.
 Metro-Goldwyn-Mayer.

Comin' at Ya (1981) Color/3-D 91 minutes
 Starring Tony Anthony, Gene Quintano, Victoria Abril, Ricardo Palacios, Gordon Lewis.
 Directed by Ferdinaco Baldi, Produced by Tony Anthony, Screenplay by Lloyd Battista, Wolf Lowenthall and Gene Quintano.
 Filmways.

The Command (1954) Color/3-D 88 minutes
Starring Guy Madison, Joan Weldon, James Whitmore, Carl Benton Reid, Harvey Lembeck, Ray Teal, Bob Nichols, Don Shelton, Gregg Barton, Boyd "Red" Morgan, Zachary Yaconelli, Renata Vanni, Tom Monroe.
Directed by David Butler, Produced by David Weisbart, Screenplay by Russell Hughes from the novel by James Warner Ballah, adapted by Samuel Fuller, Photographed by Wilfrid M. Cline, Art Direction by Bertram Tuttle, Music by Dimitri Tiomkin.
Warner Brothers.

The Crater Lake Monster (1977) Color/Fantamation 89 minutes
Starring Richard Cardella, Glenn Roberts, Mark Siegel, Bob Hyman, Richard Garrison, Kacey Cobb, Michael Hoover, Susan Lewis, Marv Eliot, Garry Johnston, Sonny Shepard, John Crowder, Susy Claycomb, Hal Scharn, Mike Simmons, and Mary Winford.
Directed and Produced by William R. Stromberg, Screenplay by William R. Stromberg, Photographed by the extremely talented Paul Gentry, Special Effects by the equally talented David Allen, Rand Cook, Phil Tippet and Tom Scherman.
Crown International (where quality goes in before the name goes on).

Creature from the Black Lagoon (1954) B&W/3-D 79 minutes
Starring Richard Carlson, Julia Adams, Richard Denning, Antonio Moreno, Nestor Paiva, Whit Bissell, Ben Chapman, Ricou Browning, Henry Excalante, Bernie Gozier, and Sidney Mason.
Directed by Jack Arnold, Produced by William Alland, Screenplay by Harry Essex and Arthur Ross from a story by Maurice Zimm, Art Direction by Bernard Herzbrun and Hilyard Brown, Makeup by Millicent Patrick and Jack Kevan, Photographed by Charles C. Welbourne, Music by Herman Stein and Hans J. Salter.
Universal-International.

The Curse of the Mummy's Tomb (1964) Color/CinemaScope 81 minutes
Starring Terence Morgan, Fred Clark, Ronal Howard, Jeanne Roland, George Pastell, Jack Gwillim, John Paul, Bernard Rabel, Dickie Owen, Michael McStay, Jill Mai Meredith, and Vernon Smythe.
Directed and Produced by Michael Carreras, Screenplay by Henry Younger, Art Direction by Bernard Robinson, Makeup by Roy Ashton, Music by Carlo Martelli.
Hammer/Columbia.

A Date with Death (1959) B&W/Psychorama 81 minutes
Starring Gerald Mohr, Liz Renay, Harry Lauter, Stephanie Farnay, Ed Erwin, Robert Clark, Red Morgan, Lew Markman, Tony Redman, Frank Bellew, William Purdy, Ray Dearholt, Melford Lehrman, and good old Ken Duncan.
Directed by Harold Daniels, Produced by William S. Edwards, Screenplay by Robert C. Dennis, Photographed by Carl Guthrie, Music by Darrell Calker.
Pacific International.

The Day of the Triffids (1963) Color/CinemaScope 95 minutes
Starring Howard Keel, Nicole Maurey, Janette Scott, Kieron Moore, Mervyn Johns, Janina Faye, Alison Leggatt, Ewan Roberts, Colette Wilde, Carole Ann Ford, Geoffrey Matthews, Gilgi Hauser, Katya Douglas, Victor Brooks, Thomas Gallagher, Sidney Vivan, Gary Hope, and John Simpson.
Directed by Steve Sekely, Produced by George Pitcher, Screenplay by Philip Yordan from the novel by John Wyndham, Photographed by Ted Moore, Art Direction by Cedric Dawe, Special Effects by Wally Veevers, Music by Ron Goodwin.
Allied Artists.

Dementia 13 (1963) B&W 81 minutes
Starring William Campbell, Luana Anders, Bart Patton, Mary Mitchel, Patrick MaGee, Ethne Dunn, Peter Read, Karl Schanzer, Ron Perry, Derry O'Donovan, and Barbara Dowling.
Directed and Screenplay by Francis Coppola, Produced by Roger Corman, Photographed by Charles Hannawalt, Music by Ronald Stein.
Filmgroup/American International.

Diamond Queen (1953) Color 80 minutes
Starring Fernando Lamas, Arlene Dahl, Gilbert Roland, Sheldon Leonard, Jay Novello, Michael Ansara, Richard Hale, Sujata and Asoka.
Directed by John Brahm, Produced by Frank Melford, Screenplay by Otto Englander, Production Designed by Eugene Lourie, Photographed by Stanley Cortez, Special Effects by Clarence Slifer, Music by Paul Sawtell.
Released by Warner Brothers.

Dracula, Prince of Darkness (1964) Color/CinemaScope 90 minutes
Starring Christopher Lee, Barbara Shelley, Andrew Keir, Francis Matthews, Suzan Farmer, Charles Tingwell, Thorley Walters, Philip Latham, Walter Brown, George Woodbridge, Jack Lambert, Philip Ray, Joyce Hemson, and John Maxim.
Directed by Terence Fisher, Produced by Anthony Nelson-Keys, Screenplay by John Sansom, Art Direction by Don Mingaye, Makeup by Roy Ashton, Music by James Bernard.
Hammer/20th Century-Fox.

Drums of Tahiti (1954) Color/3-D 73 minutes
Starring Dennis O'Keefe, Patricia Medina, Francis L. Sullivan, George Keymas, Slyvia Lewis, Cecely Browne, Raymond Lawrence, and Frances Brandt.
Directed by William Castle, Produced by Sam Katzman, Screenplay by Douglas Hayes from a story by Robert (". . . making movies is no different than making shoes") Kent, Art Direction by Paul Palmentola, Music by Mischa Bakaleinikoff.
Columbia.

Earth Vs. the Flying Saucers (1956) 83 minutes
　　Starring Hugh Marlowe, Joan Taylor, Donald Curtis, Morris Ankrum, John Zaremba, Tom Browne Henry, Grandon Rhodes, Larry Blake, Harry Lauter, Charles Evans, Clark Howat, Frank Wilcox, and Alan Reynolds.
　　Directed by Fred F. Sears, Produced by Charles H. Schneer, Screenplay by George Worthing Yates and Raymond T. Marcus from a story by Curt Siodmak suggested by "Flying Saucers from Outer Space" by Major Donald E. Keyhoe, Photographed by Fred Jackman, Jr., Art Direction by Paul Palmentola, Special Effects by Ray Harryhausen, Music by Mischa Bakaleinikoff.
　　Columbia.

Earthquake (1974) Color/Sensurround 129 minutes
　　Starring Charlton Heston, Ava Gardner, Lorne Greene, George Kennedy, Lloyd Nolan, Genevieve Bujold, Richard Roundtree, Barry Sullivan, Marjoe Gortner, Victoria Principal, Gabriel Dell, and Walter Matthau.
　　Directed and Produced by Mark Robson, Screenplay by George Fox and Mario Puzo, Music by John Williams.
　　Universal.

East of Sumatra (1953) Color 82 minutes
　　Starring Jeff Chandler, Marilyn Maxwell, Suzan Ball, Anthony Quinn, John Sutton, Jay C. Flippen, Scatman Crothers, and Aram Katcher.
　　Directed by Budd Boetticher, Produced by Albert J. Cohen, Screenplay by Frank Gill, Jr., Photographed by Clifford Stine, Art Direction by Robert Boyle, Musical Direction by Joseph Gershenson.
　　Universal-International.

The Egyptian (1954) Color/CinemaScope 144 minutes
　　Starring Jean Simmons, Victor Mature, Gene Tierney, Michael Wilding, Bella Darvi, Peter Ustinov, Edmund Purdom, Judith Evelyn, Henry Daniell, John Carradine, Carol Benton Reid, Tommy Rettig, Anita Stevens, Donna Martell, Mimi Gibson, Carmen de Lavallade, and Harry Thompson.
　　Directed by Michael Curtiz, Produced by Darryl F. Zanuck, Screenplay by Philip Dunne and Casey Robinson from the novel by Mika Waltari, Art Direction by George W. Davis, Photographed by Leon Shamroy, Special Effects by Ray Kellogg, Music by Alfred Newman and Bernard Herrmann.
　　20th Century–Fox.

The 5,000 Fingers of Dr. T (1953) Color/Wonderama 88 minutes
　　Starring Peter Lind Hayes, Mary Healy, Hans Conried, Tommy Rettig, John Heasley, Robert Heasley, Noel Cravat, and Henry Kulky.
　　Directed by Roy Rowland, Produced by Stanley Kramer, Screenplay by Dr. Seuss and Allan Scott from a story by Dr. Seuss, Photographed by Frank Planer, Art Direction by Cary Odell, Music by Frederick Hollander.
　　Columbia.

Forbidden (1953) B&W 85 minutes
Starring Tony Curtis, Joanne Dru, Lyle Bettger, Marvin Miller, Victor Sen Yung, Peter Mamakos, David Sharpe, and Alan Dexter.
Directed by Rudolph Mate, Produced by Ted Richmond, Screenplay by William Sackheim and Gil Doud, Photographed by William Daniels, Art Direction by Richard H. Riedel, Music by Frank Skinner.
Universal-International.

Forbidden Planet (1956) Color/Scope 98 minutes
Starring Walter Pidgeon, Anne Francis, Leslie Nielsen, Warren Stevens, Jack Kelly, Richard Anderson, Earl Holliman, George Wallace, Bob Dix, Jimmy Thompson, James Drury, Harry Harvey, Jr., Roger McGee, Peter Miller, Morgan Jones, Richard Grant, and Robby the Robot.
Directed by Fred McLeod Wilcox, Produced by Nicholas Nayfack, Screenplay by Cyril Hume based on a story by Irving Block and Allen Adler, Photographed by George J. Folsey, Art Direction by Cedric Gibbons and Arthur Lonergan, Special Effects by A. Arnold Gillespie, Warren Newcombe and Irving G. Ries, Electronic music by Louis and Bebe Barron.
Metro-Goldwyn-Mayer.

4-D Man (1959) Color 85 minutes
Starring Robert Lansing, Lee Meriwether, James Congdon, Robert Strauss, Edgar Stehl, and Patty Duke.
Directed by Irvin Shortess Yeaworth, Jr., Produced by Jack H. Harris, Screenplay by Theodore Simonson and Cy Chermak, Photographed by Theodore J. Pahle, Art Direction by William Jersey, Makeup by Dean Newman, Special Effects by Bert Cloane, Music by Ralph Carmichael.
Released by Universal-International.

Four Girls in Town (1956) Color/CinemaScope 85 minutes
Starring George Nader, Julie Adams, Marianne Cook, Elsa Martinelli, Gia Scala, Sydney Chaplin, Grant Williams, John Gavin, Ainslie Pryor, Helene Stanton, Herbert Anderson, Maurice Marsac, and Eugene Mazzola.
Directed and Screenplay by Jack Sher, Produced by Aaron Rosenberg, Photographed by Irving Glassberg, Art Direction by Ted Haworth, Music Supervision by Joseph Gershenson, "Rhapsody for Four Girls" composed by Alex North.
Universal-International.

Foxfire (1955) Color 92 minutes
Starring Jane Russell, Jeff Chandler, Dan Duryea, Mara Corday, Frieda Inescort, Robert F. Simon, Barton MacLane, Charlotte Wynters, Eddy C. Waller, Celia Lovsky, Arthur Space, Phil Chambers, Robert Bice, Vici Raaf, Grace Lenard, and Guy Wilkerson.
Directed by Joseph Pevney, Produced by Aaron Rosenberg, Screenplay by

Ketti Frings based on the story by Anya Seton, Photographed by William Daniels, Art Direction by Robert Clatworthy, Music by Frank Skinner. Universal-International.

Francis Joins the Wacs (1954) B&W 94 minutes
Starring Donald O'Connor, Julia Adams, Chill Wills, Mamie Van Doren, Lynn Bari, Zasu Pitts, Allison Hayes, Mara Corday, Karen Kadler, and Francis, the Talking Mule.
Directed by Arthur Lubin, Produced by Ted Richmond, Screenplay by Devery Freemean and James B. Allardice based on characters created by David Stern, Photographed by Irving Glassberg, Art Direction by Robert Clatworthy, Special Effects by David Horsley, Musical Supervision by Joseph Gershenson.
Univeral-International (naturally).

Frankenstein (1974) Color/3-D 95 minutes
Starring Joe Dallesandro, Monique van Vooren, Udo Kier, Srdjan Zelenovic, Delila Di Lazzaro, Arno Jurging, Lui Bozizio, Carla Mancini, and Marco Liofredi.
Directed and Screenplay by Paul Morrissey, Produced by Andrew Braunsberg, Art Direction by Gianni Giovagnoni, Makeup by Mario de Salvio, Special Effects by Carlo Ramisaldi, Music by Claudio Gizzi.
Brayanston Pictures.

Frankenstein Meets the Space Monster (1965) B&W 78 minutes
Starring James Karen, David Kerman, Nancy Marshall, Marilyn Hanold, Lou Cutell, and Robert Reilly.
Directed by Robert Gaffney, Produced by Robert McCarty, Screenplay by George Garret.
Released by Allied Artists.

Free, White and 21 (1963) B&W 104 minutes
Starring Frederick O'Neal, Annalena Lund, George Edgley, Johnny Hicks, and George Russell.
Directed and Produced by Larry Buchanan, Screenplay by Larry Buchanan, Harold Dwain and Cliff Pope, Photographed by Russell K. Johnson, Art Direction by Derwin Adams.
American International.

The French Line (1954) Color/3-D 102 minutes
Starring Jane Russell, Gilbert Roland, Arthur Hunnicutt, Mary McCarty, Joyce MacKenzie, Paul Corday, Scott Elliot, Craig Stevens, Laura Elliot, Steven Geray, John Wangraf, Michael St. Angel, Barbara Darrow, Clarence Darrow, and Ann Darrow.
Directed by Lloyd Bacon, Produced by Edmund Grainger, Screenplay by Mary Loos and Richard Sale from a story by Matty Remp and Isabel Dawn, Art Direction by Albert D'Agostino and Carroll Clark.
RKO.

Girl in the Kremlin (1957) B&W 81 minutes
Starring Lex Barker, Zsa Zsa Gabor, Jeffrey Stone, Maurice Manson, William Schallert, Aram Katcher, Natalia Daryll, and Michael Fox.
Directed by Russell Birdwell, Produced by Albert Zugsmith, Screenplay by Gene L. Coon and Robert Hill, Photographed by Carl Gurthrie, Art Direction by Eric Orbom, Music Supervision by Joseph Gershenson.
Universal-International.

Girls on the Loose (1958) B&W 78 minutes
Starring Mara Corday, Lita Milan, Barbara Bostock, Mark Richman, Joyce Barker, and Abby Dalton.
Directed by Paul Henreid, Produced by Harry Rybnick and Richard Kay, Screenplay by Alan Friedman and Dorothy Raison and Allen Rivkin, Photographed by Philip Lathrop, Art Direction by Robert E. Smith, Songs by Jay Livingston and Ray Evans.
Universal-International.

Gog (1954) Color/3-D 85 minutes
Starring Richard Egan, Constance Dowling, Herbert Marshall, John Wengraf, Philip Van Zandt, Valerie Vernon, Steve Roberts, Byron Kane, David Alpert, Michael Fox, and William Schallert.
Directed by Herbert L. Strock, Produced by Ivan Tors, Screenplay by Tom Taggart from a story by Ivan Tors, Art Direction by William Ferrari, Music by Harry Sukman.
United Artists.

Gunsmoke (1953) Color 79 minutes
Starring Audie Murphy, Susan Cabot, Paul Kelly, Charles Drake, Mary Castle, Jack Kelly, Jesse White, and William Reynolds.
Directed by Nathan Juran, Produced by Aaron Rosenberg, Screenplay by D.D. Beauchamp, Photographed by Charles P. Boyle, Art Direction by Robert F. Boyle, Musical Direction by Joseph Gershenson.

The Gorgon (1964) Color 83 minutes
Starring Peter Cushing, Christopher Lee, Richard Pasco, Michael Goodliffe, and Barbara Shelley.
Directed by Terence Fisher, Produced by Anthony Nelson-Keys, Screenplay by John Gilling based on a story by J. Llewellyn Devine, Art Direction by Bernard Robinson, Makeup by Roy Ashton, Music by James Bernard.
Hammer/Columbia.

The H-Man (1959) Color 79 minutes
Starring Yumi Shirakawa, Kenji Sahara, Skiniko Hirata, Eitaro Ozawa, Koreya Senda, and Mitsuru Sato.
Directed by Inoshiro Honda, Produced by Tomouuki Tanaka, Screenplay

by Takeshi Kimura from a story by Hideo Kaijo, Photographed by Hajime Koizumi, Art Direction by Takeo Kita, Special Effects by Eiji Tsuburaya, Music by Masaru Sato.
Toho/Columbia.

He Walked by Night (1948) B&W 79 minutes
Starring Richard Basehart, Scott Brady, Roy Roberts, Whit Bissell, Jim Cardwell, Jack Webb, and Felice Ingersol.
Directed by Alfred Werker, Produced by Robert T. Kane, Screenplay by John C. Higgins and Crane Wilbur with additional dialog by Harry Essex from an original story by Crane Wilbur, Photographed by John Alton, Art Direction by Edward Ilou, Special Effects by Jack Rabin, Music by Irving Friedman.
Eagle Lion.

Hey, Let's Twist! (1961) B&W 80 minutes
Starring Joe Dee and the Starliters, Jo-Ann Campbell, Teddy Randazzo, Kay Armen, Zohra Lampert, Dino di Luca, The Peppermint Loungers, and Alan Arbus.
Directed by Greg Garrison, Produced by Harry Romm, Screenplay by Hal Hackady, Photographed by George Jacobson, Art Direction by Al Brenner.
Paramount.

Homicidal (1961) B&W 87 minutes
Starring Glenn Corbett, Patricia Breslin, Jean Arless, Eugenie Leontovich, Alan Bunce, Richard Rust, Jame Westerfield, Gilbert Green, Wolfe Barzell, Hope Summers, Teri Brooks, Ralph Moody, and Joe Forte.
Directed and Produced by William Castle, Screenplay by Robb White, Photographed by Burnett Guffey, Art Direction by Cary Odell, Makeup by Ben Lane, Music by Hugo Friedhofer.
Columbia.

Hondo (1954) Color/3-D 84 minutes
Starring John Wayne, Geraldine Page, Ward Bond, Michael Pate, James Arness, Rodolfo Acosta, Leo Gordon, Tom Irish, Lee Aker, Paul Fix, and Rayford Barnes.
Directed by John Farrow, Produced by Robert Fellows, Screenplay by James Edward Grant from the novel by Louis L'Amour, Art Direction by Al Yberra, Music by Emil Newman and Hugo Friedhofer.
Released by Warner Brothers.

The Horror of Party Beach (1964) B&W 72 minutes
Starring John Scott, Alice Lyon, Allen Laurel, Eulabelle Moore, Marilyn Clark, Agustin Mayer, Damon Klebroyd, Monroe Wade, Carol Grubman, Dina Harris, Emily Laurel, Sharon Murphy, Diane Prizio, and the ever-popular Del-Aires.

Directed and Produced by Del Tenney, Screenplay by Richard L. Hilliard, Art Direction by Robert Verberkmoss, Music by Bill Holmes.
Released by 20th Century–Fox.

Horrors of the Black Museum (1959) Color/Scope/HypnoVista 94 minutes
Starring Michael Gough, June Cunningham, Graham Curnow, Shirley Ann Field, Geoffrey Keen, Gerald Andersen, John Warwick, Beatrice Varley, Austin Trevor, Malou Panera, Howard Greene, Dorinda Stevens, Stuart Saunders, Hilda Barry, and Nora Gordon.
Directed by Arthur Crabtree, Produced by Herman Cohen, Screenplay by Kandel and Herman Cohen, Art Direction by Wilfred Arnold, Makeup by Geoffrey Muller, Music by Gerard Schumann.
American International.

House of Wax (1953) Color/3-D 88 minutes
Starring Vincent Price, Frank Lovejoy, Phyllis Kirk, Carloyn Jones, Paul Picerni, Roy Roberts, Angela Clarke, Paul Cavanagh, Dabbs Greer, Charles Buchinsky (Bronson), Reggie Rymal, and Philip Tonge.
Directed by Andre de Toth, Produced by Bryan Foy, Screenplay by Crane Wilbur from a story by Charles Belden, Photographed by Bert Glennon and Peverell Marley, Art Direction by Stanley Fleischer, Makeup by Gordon Bau, Music by David Buttolph.
Warner Brothers.

House on Haunted Hill (1959) B&W/Emergo 75 minutes
Starring Vincent Price, Carol Ohmart, Richard Long, Alan Marshal, Carolyn Craig, Elisha (boy how he can) Cook, Julie Mitchum, Leon Anderson, and Howard Hoffman.
Directed and Produced by William Castle, Screenplay by Robb White, Photographed by Carl E. Guthrie, Art Direction by David Milton, Special Effects by Herman Townsley, Makeup by Jack Dusick, Music by Von Dexter.
Allied Artists.

How the West Was Won (1963) Color/Cinerama 155 minutes
Starring Carroll Baker, Lee J. Cobb, Henry Fonda, Carolyn Jones, Karl Malden, Gregory Peck, George Peppard, Robert Preston, Debbie Reynolds, James Stewart, Eli Wallach, John Wayne, Richard Widmark, Brigid Bazlen, Walter Brennan, David Brian, Andy Devine, Raymond Massey, Agnes Moorehead, Henry (Harry) Morgan, Thelma Ritter, Mickey Shaughnessy, Russ Tamblyn, narrated by Spencer Tracy.
Directed by John Ford, George Marshall, Henry Hathaway, Produced by Bernard Smith, Screenplay by James R. Webb, Photographed by William H. Daniels, Milton Krasner, Charles Lang, Jr., and Joseph LaShelle, Special Effects by A. Arnold Gillespie and Robert R. Hoag, Art Direction by George W. Davis, Music by Alfred Newman.
Metro-Goldwyn-Mayer.

How to Marry a Millionaire (1953) Color/Scope 95 minutes
Starring Betty Grable, Marilyn Monroe, Lauren Bacall, David Wayne, Rory Calhoun, Cameron Mitchell, Alex D'Arcy, Fred Clark, William Powell, George Dunn, Percy Helton, Robert Adler, Harry Carter, Tudor Owen, Maurice Marsac, Emmett Vogen, and Hermine Sterler.
Directed by Jean Negulesco, Produced and Screenplay by Nunnally Johnson, Art Direction by Lyle Wheeler and Leland Fuller, Music by Alfred Newman.
20th Century–Fox.

The Hypnotic Eye (1959) B&W/HypnoMagic 79 minutes
Starring Jacques Bergerac, Allison Hayes, Marcia Henderson, Merry Anders, Joe Patridge, Guy Prescott, James Lydon, Phyllis Colo, Carol Thurston, Holly Harris, Mary Foran, Ferdinand (Fred) W. Demara,* Lawrence Lipton, and Eric (Big Daddy) Nord.
Directed by George Blair, Produced by Charles B. Bloch, Screenplay by Gitta and William Read Woodfield, Art Direction by David Milton, Special Effects by Milton Olsen, Makeup by Emile La Vigne, Music by Marlin Skiles.
Allied Artists.

I Dismember Mama (1972) Color 81 minutes
Starring Zooey Hall, Geri Reischl, Joanne Moore Jordan, Greg Mullavey, and Marlene Tracy.
Directed by Paul Leder, Produced by Leon Roth, Photographed by William Swenning, Music by Herschel Burke Gilbert.
Europix International.

It Came from Outer Space (1953) B&W/3-D 81 minutes
Starring Richard Carlson, Barbara Rush, Charles Drake, Russell Johnson, Kathleen Hughes, Joseph Sawyer, Dave Wilcock, and Alan Dexter.
Directed by Jack Arnold, Produced by William Alland, Screenplay by Harry Essex from Ray Bradbury's 80 page treatment, Art Direction by Bernard Herzbrun and Robert Boyle, Special Effects by David S. Horsley, Music by Herman Stein.
Universal-International.

It Conquered the World (1956) B&W 71 minutes
Starring Peter Graves, Beverly Garland, Lee Van Cleef, Sally Fraser, Russ Bender, Jonathan Haze, Dick Miller, Charles Griffith, Karen Kadler, and Paul Blaisdell.
Directed and Produced by Roger Corman, Screenplay by Lou Rusoff and

Fred Demara was the subject of a book by Robert Crichton titled The Great Imposter *which was eventually made into a movie. Demara appeared on network television and confessed that he'd posed as a doctor, a college professor, and a prison warden among other things.*

Charles B. Griffith, Photographed by Frederick West, Special Effects by Paul Blaisdell, Music by Ronald Stein.

American International.

I, the Jury (1953) B&W/3-D 87 minutes

Starring Biff Elliot, Preston Foster, Peggie Castle, Margaret Sheridan, Alan Reed, Frances Osborne, Robert Cunningham, Elisha Cook, Jr., Paul Dubov, Mary Anderson, Dran Seitz, Tani Seitz, Robert Swanger, and John Qualen.

Directed and Screenplay by Harry Essex from the novel by Mickey Spillane, Produced by Victor Saville, Art Direction by Wiard Ihnen, Music by Franz Waxman.

United Artists.

It! The Terror from Beyond Space (1958) B&W 68 minutes

Starring Marshall Thompson, Shawn Smith, Kim Spalding, Ann Doran, Dabbs Greer, Paul Langton, Robert Bice, Richard Harvey, Richard Benedict, Thom Carney, and Ray "Crash" Corrigan.

Directed by Edward L. Cahn, Produced by Robert E. Kent, Screenplay by Jerome Bixby, Art Direction by William Gladgow, Special Effects by Paul Blaisdell, Music by Paul Sawtell and Bert Shefter.

United Artists.

Jack, the Giant Killer (1962) Color/Fantascope 94 minutes

Starring Kerwin Mathews, Judi Meredith, Torin Thatcher, Walter Burke, Roger Mobley, Barry Kelley, Don Beddoe, Dayton Lummis, Anna Lee, and Helen Wallace.

Directed by Nathan Juran, Produced by Edward Small, Screenplay by Orville H. Hampton and Nathan Juran from a story by Orville H. Hampton, Photographed by David S. Horsley, Art Direction by Fernando Carrere and Frank McCoy, Special Effects by Howard Anderson, Jim Danforth, and Gene Warren, Music by Paul Sawtell and Bert Shefter.

United Artists.

Jivaro (1954) Color/3-D 91 minutes

Starring Fernando Lamas, Rhonda Fleming, Brian Keith, Lon Chaney, Jr., Richard Denning, Rita Moreno, Marvin Miller, Morgan Farley, Pascual Pena, Nestor Paiva, and Charlie Lung.

Directed by Edward Ludwig, Produced by William H. Pine and William C. Thomas, Screenplay by Winston Miller from a story by David Duncan, Art Direction by Earl Hedrick, Special Effects by John P. Fulton, Music by Gregory Stone.

Paramount.

Jungle Moon Men (1955) Sepia 70 minutes
    Starring Johnny Weissmuller, Jean Byron, Helene Stanton, Bill Henry, Myron Healey, Billy Curtis, Michael Granger, Frank Sully, Benjamin F. Chapman, Jr., Kenneth L. Smith, and Ed Hinton.
    Directed by Charles S. Gould, Produced by Sam Katzman, Screenplay by Dwight V. Babcock and Jo Pagano, Photographed by Henry Freulich, Art Direction by Paul Palmentola, Special Effects by Jack Erickson, Music Conducted by Mischa Bakaleinikoff.
    Columbia.

The Kettles on Old MacDonald's Farm (1957) B&W 80 minutes
    Starring Marjorie Main, Parker Fennelly, Gloria Talbott, John Smith, George Dunn, and Roy Barcroft.
    Directed by Virgil Vogel, Produced by Howard Christie, Screenplay by William Raynor and Herbert Margolis, Photographed by Arthur E. Arling, Art Direction by Alexander Golitzen and Philip Barber, Special Effects by Clifford Stine, Music Supervision by Joseph Gershenson.
    Universal-International.

The King and I (1956) Color/CinemaScope 133 minutes
    Starring Deborah Kerr, Yul Brynner, Rita Moreno, Terry Saunders, Carlos Rivas, Rex Thomson, and Alan Mowbray.
    Directed by Walter Lang, Produced by Charles Brackett, Screenplay by Ernest Lehman from the play by Richard Rodgers and Oscar Hammerstein II based on the novel "Anna and the King of Siam" by Margaret Landon, Photographed by Charles Lang, Music by Alfred Newman.
    20th Century–Fox.

Kiss Me Kate (1954) Color/3-D 109 minutes
    Starring Kathryn Grayson, Howard Keel, Ann Miller, Keenan Wynn, Bobby Van, Tommy Rall, James Whitmore, Kurt Kasznar, Bob Fosse, Ron Randell, Willard Parker, Dave O'Brien, Claud Allister, Ann Codee, Carol Haney, and Jeanne Coyne.
    Directed by George Sidney, Produced by Jack Cummings, Screenplay by Dorothy Kingsley based on the play by Samuel and Bella Spewack, Art Direction by Cedric Gibbons and Urie McCleary, Special Effects by Warren Newcombe, Music by Cole Porter, Orchestrations by Conrad Salinger and Skip Martin.
    Metro-Goldwyn-Mayer.

Knights of the Round Table (1954) Color/CinemaScope 115 minutes
    Starring Robert Taylor, Ava Gardner, Mel Ferrer, Anne Crawford, Stanley Baker, Felix Aylmer, Maureen Swanson, Gabriel Woolf, Anthony Forwood, and Robert Urquehart.
    Directed by Richard Thorpe, Produced by Pandro S. Berman, Screenplay by Talbot Jennings, Jan Lustig, and Noel Langley based on "le Morte D'Arthur"

by Sir Thomas Malory, Art Direction by Alfred Jungle and Hans Peters, Special Effects by Tom Howard, Music by Miklos Rosza.
Metro-Goldwyn-Mayer.

Land of Fury (1955) Color 90 minutes
Starring Jack Hawkins, Glynnis Johns, Noel Purcell, Laui Raki, India Te Wiata, Kenneth Williams, Patrick Warbrick, and Tony Erstich.
Directed by Ken Annakin, Produced by George H. Brown, Screenplay by William Fairchild.
Universal-International.

The Lost Missile (1958) B&W 71 minutes
Starring Robert Loggia, Ellen Parker, Larry Kerr, Marilee Earle, Philip Pine, Fred Engleberg, Kitty Kelly, Selmer Jackson, Joe Hyams, Bill Bradley, and Lawrence Dobkin.
Directed by Lester William Berke, Produced by Lee Gordon, Screenplay by John McPartland and Jerome Bixby from a story by Lester William Berke, Photographed by Kenneth Peach, Art Direction by William Ferrari, Special Effects by Jack R. Glass, Music by Gerald Fried.
A United Artists Release.

The Lost Weekend (1945) B&W 101 minutes
Starring Ray Milland, Jane Wyman, Philip Terry, Howard da Silva, Doris Dowling, Frank Faylen, Mary Young, Anita Bolster, Lilian Fontaine, Lewis L. Russell, and Frank Orth.
Directed by Billy Wilder, Produced by Charles Brackett, Screenplay by Charles Brackett and Billy Wilder from the novel by Charles Jackson, Photographed by John P. Seitz, Art Direction by Hans Dreier and Earl Hedrick, Special Effects by Gordon Jennings, Music by Miklos Rozsa.
Paramount.

Louisiana Territory (1954) Color/3-D 65 minutes
Starring Val Winter, Leo Zinser, Julian Meister, Phyliss Massicot, and Marlene Behrens.
Directed by Harry W. Smith, Produced by Jay Bonafield and Douglas Travers, Screenplay by Jerome Brondfield.
RKO.

Macabre (1958) B&W 73 minutes
Starring William Prince, Jim Backus, Jacqueline Scott, Philip Tongue, Ellen Corby, Susan Morrow, Christine White, Linda Guderman, Jonathan Kidd, Dorothy Morris, and Howard Hoffman.
Directed and Produced by William Castle, Screenplay by Robb White from the novel "The Marble Orchard" by Theo Durrant, Photographed by Carl E. Guthrie, Art Direction by Jack T. Collis and Robert Kinoshita, Makeup by Jack Dusick, Special Effects by Jack Rabin, Louis Dewitt and Irving Block, Music by Les Baxter.
Allied Artists.

Mad Doctor of Blood Island (1969) Color 85 minutes
Starring John Ashley, Angelique Pettyjohn, Ronald Peary, Alicia Alonzo, and Ronoldo Valdez.
Directed by Geraldo de Leon and Eddie Romero, Produced by Eddie Romero, Screenplay by Reuben Conway.
Hemisphere.

The Mad Magician (1953) B&W/3-D 72 minutes
Starring Vincent Price, Mary Murphy, Eva Gabor, John Emery, Donald Randolph, Lenita Lane, Patrick O'Neal, and Jay Novello.
Directed by John Brahm, Produced by Bryan Foy, Screenplay by Crane Wilbur, Photographed by Bert Glennon, Art Direction by Frank Sylos, Special Effects by David Koehler, Makeup by Gustaf Norin and George Bau, Music by Emil Newman and Arthur Lange.
Columbia.

Man in the Dark (1953) B&W/3-D 70 minutes
Starring Edmond O'Brien, Audrey Totter, Ruth Warren, Ted de Corsia, and Horace McMahon.
Directed by Lew Landers, Produced by Wallace MacDonald, Screenplay by George Bricker and Jack Leonard based on "The Man Who Lived Twice" by Tom Van Dyke, Fred Niblo, Jr., and Arthur Strawn, Music by Mischa Bakleinikoff.
Columbia.

The Mask (1961) B&W/3-D 83 minutes
Starring Paul Stevens, Claudette Nevins, Bill Walker, Anne Collings, Martin Lavut, Leo Leyden, Eleanor Beecroft, William Bryden, Norman Ettlinger, Stephen Appleby, Ray Lawlor, Jim Moran, Nancy Island, Rudi Linschoten, and Paul Nevins.
Directed and Produced by Julian Roffman, Screenplay by Frank Taubes and Sandy Haber, Photographed by Herbert S. Alpert and Charles W. Smith, Special Effects by Herman S. Townsley and James B. Gordon, Art Direction by David S. Ballou, Music by Louis Applebaum.
A Warner Brothers Release.

Miss Sadie Thompson (1954) Color/3-D 91 minutes
Starring Rita Hayworth, Jose Ferrer, Aldo Ray, Russell Collins, Diosa Costello, Harry Bellaver, Wilton Graff, Peggy Converse, Henry Slate, Rudy Bond, Charles Buchinsky (Bronson), Frances Morris, Peter Chong, and John Grossett.
Directed by Curtis Bernhardt, Produced by Jerry Wald, Screenplay by Harry Kleiner from the story by Somerset Maugham, Art Direction by Carl Anderson.
Columbia.

Mr. Sardonicus (1961) B&W 89 minutes
Starring Oscar Homolka, Ronald Lewis, Audrey Dalton, Guy Rolfe, Vladimir Sokoloff, Erika Peters, Lorna Hanson, James Forrest, Tina Woodward, Constance Cavendish, Mavis Neal, Charles Hradiklak, David Janti, Franz Roehn, Annalena Lund, Ilse Burkert, and Albert d'Arno.
Directed and Produced by William Castle, Screenplay by Ray Russel, Photographed by Burnett Guffrey, Art Direction by Cary Odell, Makeup by Ben Lane, Music by Von Dexter.
Columbia.

Monkey on My Back (1957) B&W 94 minutes
Starring Cameron Mitchell, Dianne Foster, Paul Richards, Jack Albertson, Kathy Garver, Lisa Golm, Barry Kelley, Dayton Lummis, Lewis Charles, Raymond Greenleaf, Richard Benedict, Brad Harris, and Robert Holton.
Directed by Andre de Toth, Produced by Edward Small, Screenplay by Crane Wilbur, Anthony Veiler and Paul Dudley, Photographed by Maury Gertsman, Art Direction by Frank Hotaling, Music by Paul Sawtell and Bert Shefter.
A United Artists Release.

The Naked Dawn (1955) Color 82 minutes
Starring Arthur Kennedy, Betta St. John, Eugene Iglesias, Charlita, and Roy Engel.
Directed by Edgar G. Ulmer, Produced by James O. Radford, Screenplay by Nina and Herman Schneider, Photographed by Frederick Gately, Art Direction by Martin Lencer, Special Effects by Jack R. Glass, Music by Herschel Burke Gilbert.
Universal-International.

Napoleon (1927) B&W/Cinerama 235 minutes
Starring Vladimir Roudenko, Albert Dieudonne, Mme. Gina Manes, Nicolas Koline, Alexandre Koubitzky, Antonia Artaud, Edmond Van Daele, and Harry Krimer.
Directed by Abel Gance, Assistant Direction by Henry Krauss, Vladimir Tourjansky, Andre Andreani, Alexandre Vokoff, Marius Nalpass, Pierre Danis and Anatole Litvak, Art Direction by Alexandre Benas, Schildknecht, Lochavoff, Jacouty, Meinhardt, and Eugene Lourie.

The Nebraskan (1954) Color/3-D 68 minutes
Starring Phil Carey, Roberta Haynes, Wallace Ford, Richard Webb, Lee Van Cleef, Regis Toomey, Jay Silverheels, Pat Hogan, Dennis Weaver, Boyd Morgan, and Frankie Fane.
Directed by Fred F. Sears, Produced by Wallace MacDonald, Screenplay by David Lang and Martin (everybody's a commie but me) Berkeley from a story by David Lamb, Art Direction by Robert Peterson, Music by Ross Di Maggio.
Columbia.

Night Walker (1964) Color 96 minutes

Starring Robert Taylor, Barbara Stanwyck, Lloyd Bochner, Judith Meredith, Hayden Roarke, Rochelle Hudson, Marjorie Bennett, Jess Barker, Paulle Clark, and Tetsu Komai.

Directed and Produced by William Castle, Screenplay by Robert Bloch, Photographed by Harold Stine, Art Direction by Frank Arrigo, Special Effects by Charles Spurgeon, Makeup by Carl Silvera and Dick Blair, Music by Vic Mizzy.

Universal.

Oklahoma (1956) Color/Todd AO 145 minutes

Starring Gordon MacRae, Shirley Jones, Gloria Grahame, Gene Nelson, Charlotte Greenwood, James Whitmore, Rod Steiger, Jay C. Flippen, and Steven Ritch as The Werewolf.

Directed by Fred Zinnemann, Produced by Arthur Hornblow, Jr., Screenplay by Oscar Hammerstein II, Music by Richard Rodgers.

United Artists.

The Old Dark House (1963) Color 86 minutes

Starring Tom Poston, Robert Morley, Janette Scott, Joyce Grenfell, Mervyn Johns, Fenella Fielding, Peter Bull, Danny Green, and John Harvey.

Directed by William Castle, Produced by William Castle and Anthony Hinds, Screenplay by Robert Dillon based on the novel by J.B. Priestley, Photographed by Arthur Grant, Special Effects by Les Bowie, Makeup by Roy Ashton.

Hammer/Columbia.

Our Man Flint (1966) Color/CinemaScope 108 minutes

Starring James Coburn, Lee J. Cobb, Gila Golan, Edward Mulhare, Benson Fond, Gianna Serra, Sigrid Valdis, Shelby Frant, Helen Funai, Michael St. Clair, Rhys Williams, Russ Conway, Ena Hartman, William Walker, Peter Brocco, Steven Geray, and Alberto Morin.

Directed by Daniel Mann, Produced by Saul David, Screenplay by Hal Fibberg and Ben Starr from a story by Hal Fibberg, Photographed by Daniel L. Fapp, Art Direction by Jack Martin Smith and Ed Graves, Special Effects by L.B. Abbott, Howard Lydecker and Emil Kosa, Jr., Music by Jerry Goldsmith.

20th Century–Fox.

Phantom of the Rue Morgue (1954) Color/3-D 84 minutes

Starring Karl Malden, Claude Dauphin, Patricia Medina, Steve Forrest, Allyn McLerie, Veola Vonn, Dolores Dorn, Anthony Caruso, Merv Griffin, Paul Richards, Rolphe Sedan, Erin O'Brien-Moore, and The Flying Zucchinis.

Directed by Roy Del Ruth, Produced by Henry Blanke, Screenplay by

Harold Medford and James R. Webb from Edgar Allan Poe's "Murders in the Rue Morgue," Photographed by J. Peverell Marley, Art Direction by Bertram Tuttle, Music by David Buttolph.
Warner Brothers.

Polyester (1981) Color/Odorama 86 minutes
Starring Tab Hunter, Divine (Glenn Milstead), Edith Massey, Mary Garlington, Ken King, David Samson, Mink Stole, and Stiv Bators.
Directed, Produced, and Screenplay by John Waters.
New Line.

The Price of Fear (1956) B&W 79 minutes
Starring Merle O'Berson, Lex Barker, Charles Drake, Gia Scala, Warren Stevens, Mary Field, Tim Sullivan, Phil Pine, Dan Riff, Stafford Repp, and Konstantin Shayne.
Directed by Abner Biberman, Produced by Howard Christie, Screenplay by Robert Tallman, Photographed by Irving Glassberg, Art Direction by Robert Clatworthy, Music Supervision by Joseph Gershenson.
Universal-International.

Psycho (1960) B&W 109 minutes
Starring Anthony Perkins, Vera Miles, John Gavin, Martin Balsam, John McIntire, Simon Oakland, Janet Leigh, Frank Albertson, Pat Hitchcock, Vaughn Taylor, Laurene Tuttle, John Anderson, and Mort Mills.
Directed and Produced by Alfred Hitchcock, Screenplay by Joseph Stefano based on the novel by Robert Bloch, Photographed by John L. Russell, Art Direction by Robert Clatworthy, Music by Bernard Herrmann.
Paramount.

Rasputin—The Mad Monk (1966) Color/Scope 92 minutes
Starring Christopher Lee, Barbara Shelley, Richard Pasco, Francis Matthews, Suzan Farmer, Dinsdale Landen, Renee Asherson, Derek Francis, Alan Tilvern, Joss Ackland, John Welsh, Robert Duncan, and John Bailey.
Directed by Don Sharp, Produced by Anthony Nelson-Keys, Screenplay by John Elder, Photographed by Michael Reed, Art Direction by Don Mingaye, Makeup by Roy Ashton, Music by Don Banks.
Hammer/20th Century–Fox.

Raw Edge (1956) Color 76 minutes
Starring Rory Calhoun, Yvonne De Carlo, Mara Corday, Rex Reason, Neville Brand, Emile Meyer, Herbert Rudley, and Robert Wilkie.
Directed by John Sherwood, Produced by Albert Zugsmith, Screenplay by Harry Essex and Robert Hill, Photographed by Maury Gertsman, Art Direction by Alfred Sweeney, Music Supervision by Joseph Gershenson.
Universal-International.

The Restless Years (1958) B&W/Scope 86 minutes
Starring John Saxon, Sandra Dee, Luana Patten, Margaret Lindsay, Virginia Grey, Teresa Wright, Alan Baxter, James Whitmore, Dorothy Green, and Jody McCrea.
Directed by Helmut Kautner, Produced by Ross Hunter, Screenplay by Edward Anhalt based on the play by "Teach Me How to Cry" by Patricia Joudry (Steele), Photographed by Ernest Laszlo, Art Direction by Philip Barber, Music by Frank Skinner.
Universal-International.

Revenge of the Creature (1955) B&W/3-D 82 minutes
Starring John Agar, Lori Nelson, John Bromfield, Robert B. Williams, Nestor Paiva, Grandon Rhodes, Dave Willock, Charles Cane, and Clint Eastwood.
Directed by Jack Arnold, Produced by William Alland, Screenplay by Martin Berkeley, Photographed by Charles S. Welbourne, Art Direction by Alfred Sweeney, Makeup by Bud (taking all the credit) Westmore, Music by Frank Skinner.
Universal-International.

The Robe (1953) Color/CinemaScope 135 minutes
Starring Richard Burton, Jean Simmons, Victor Mature (a.k.a. extremely handsome Tony Powell), Michael Rennie, Richard Boone, Jeff Morrow, Dawn Adams, and Dean Jagger.
Directed by Henry Koster, Produced by Frank Ross, Screenplay by Philip Donne from the novel by Lloyd C. Douglas, Music by Alfred Newman.
20th Century–Fox.

Robot Monster (1953) B&W/3-D 62 minutes
Starring George Nader, Claudia Barret, John Mylong, Selena Royle, Pamela Paulson, George Barrows, and Gregory Moffett.
Directed by Phil Tucker, Produced by Al Zimbalist, Screenplay by Wyott Ordung, Special Effects by Jack Rabin and David Commons, Music by Elmer Bernstein.
Astor.

Running Wild (1955) B&W 81 minutes
Starring William Campbell, Mamie Van Doren, Keenan Wynn, Kathleen Case, Jan Merlin, John Saxon, Chris Randall, Walter Coy, Sumner Williams, and Mike Fox.
Directed by Abner Biberman, Produced by Howard Pine, Screenplay by Leo Townsend from a novel by Ben Benson, Photographed by Ellis W. Carter, Art Direction by Robert Boyle, Music Supervision by Joseph Gershenson.
Universal-International.

Sangaree (1953) Color/3-D 94 minutes

Starring Fernando Lamas, Arlene Dahl, Patricia Medina, Francis L. Sullivan, Charles Korvin, Tom Drake, John Sutton, Willard Parker, and Lester Matthews.

Directed by Edward Ludwig, Produced by William H. Pine, Screenplay by David Duncan from the novel by Frank G. Slaughter, adapted by Frank Moss, Art Direction by Earl Hedrick.

Paramount.

Scent of Mystery (1960) Color/Smell-O-Vision

Starring Peter Lorre, Diana Dors, Denholm Elliott, Paul Lukas, and Leo McKern.

Directed by Jack Cardiff, Produced by Michael Todd, Jr., Screenplay by William Roos.

Scent of Mystery Productions.

The Screaming Skull (1958) B&W 70 (long) minutes

Starring John Hudson, Peggy Webber, Toni Johnson, Russ Conway, and Alex Nicol.

Directed by Alex Nicol, Produced and Screenplay by John Kneubuhl, Photographed by Frank Crosley, Makeup by Don Robertson, Music by Ernest Gold.

American International.

Second Chance (1953) Color/3-D 82 minutes

Starring Robert Mitchum, Linda Darnell, Jack Palance, Sandro Giglio, Rodolfo Hoyos, Jr., Reginald Sheffield, Margaret Brewster, Roy Roberts, Salvador Baguez, Maurice Jara, Judy Walsh, Dan Seymour, Fortunio Bonanova, Milburn Stone, and Abel Frenandez.

Directed by Rudolph Mate, Produced by Sam Weisenthal, Screenplay by Oscar Millard and Sydney Boehm, Photographed by William Snyder, Art Direction by Albert S. DiAgostino and Carroll Clark, Music by Roy Webb.

RKO Radio Pictures, Inc.

Secret File Hollywood (1962) B&W 85 minutes

Starring Robert Clarke, Francine York, Syd Mason, Maralou Gray, and John Warburton.

Directed by Ralph Cushman, Produced by Rudolph Cusumano and James Dyer, Screenplay by Jack Lewis, Photographed by Gregory Sandor.

Crown International.

Seven Brides for Seven Brothers (1954) Color/CinemaScope 103 minutes

Starring Jane Powell, Howard Keel, Jeff Richards, Russ Tamblyn, Tommy Rall, Virginia Gibson, Julie Newmeyer, Matt Mattox, Jack D'Amboise, and Marc Platt.

Directed by Stanley Donen, Produced by Jack Cummings, Screenplay by Albert Hackett and Frances Goodrich loosely based on Stephen Vincent Benet's "The Sobbin' Women," Choreographed by Michael Kidd, Music by Johnny Mercer and Gene de Paul.
Metro-Goldwyn-Mayer.

The Seventh Voyage of Sinbad (1958) Color/Dynamation 94 minutes
Starring Kerwin Mathews, Kathryn Grant, Torin Thatcher, and Richard Eyer.
Directed by Nathan Juran, Produced by Charles H. Schneer, Screenplay by Kenneth Kolb, Special Effects by Ray Harryhausen, Photographed by Wilkie Cooper, Music by Bernard Herrmann.
Columbia.

Sinbad and the Eye of the Tiger (1977) Color/Dynarama 113 minutes
Starring Patrick Wayne, Taryn Power, Margaret Whiting, Jane Seymour, Patrick Troughton, Kurt Christian, Nadim Sawalha, Damien Thomas, Bruno Barnabe, Bernard Kay, Salami Coker, and David Sterne.
Directed by Sam Wanamaker, Produced by Charles H. Schneer and Ray Harryhausen, Screenplay by (yawn) Beverly Cross from a story by Beverly Cross and Ray Harryhausen, Photographed by Ted Moore, Special Effects by Ray Harryhausen.
Columbia.

Singin' in the Rain (1952) Color 102 minutes
Starring Gene Kelly, Donald O'Connor, Debbie Reynolds, Jean Hagen, Millard Mitchell, Cyd Charisse, Rita Moreno, Douglas Fowley, and Madge Blake.
Directed by Gene Kelly and Stanley Donen, Produced by Arthur Freed, Screenplay by Betty Comden and Adolph Green, Photographed by Harold Rosson, Songs and Lyrics by Arthur Freed, Special Effects by Warren Newcombe, Music by Nacio Herb Brown.
Metro-Goldwyn-Mayer.

Slim Carter (1957) Color 82 minutes
Starring Jock Mahoney, Julie Adams, Tim Hovey, William Hopper, Ben Johnson, Joanna Moore, Walter Reed, Maggie Mahoney, Roxanne Arlen, Jim Healy, Bill Williams, and Barbara Hale.
Directed by Richard H. Bartlett, Produced by Howie Horwitz, Screenplay by Montgomery Pittman from a story by David Bramson and Mary C. McCall, Jr., Photographed by Ellis W. Carter, Art Direction by Eric Orbom, Music by Herman Stein.
Universal-International.

A Star Is Born (1938) Color 111 minutes
Starring Janet Gaynor, Fredric March, Adolph Menjou, May Robson, Andy Devine, Lionel Stander, Elizabeth Jenns, Edgar Kennedy, Owen Moore, J.C. Nugent, Clara Blandick, A.W. Sweatt, Peggy Wood, Adrian Rosely, Arthur Hout, Guinn Williams, Vince Barnett, Paul Stanton, and Franklin Pangborn.
Directed by William A. Wellman, Produced by David O. Selznick, Screenplay by Dorothy Parker, Alan Campbell, and Robert Carson from a story by William A. Wellman and Robert Carson, Photographed by W. Howard Greene, Special Effects by Jack Cosgrove, Music by Max Steiner.
United Artists.

The Story of Alexander Graham Bell (1939) B&W 97 minutes
Starring Don Ameche, Loretta Young, Henry Fonda, Charles Coburn, Gene Lockhart, Spring Byington, Sally Blane, Polly Ann Young, Georgiana Young, Bobs Watson, Russell Hicks, Paul Stanton, Jonathan Hale, Harry Davenport, Elizabeth Patterson, Charles Trowbridge, Jan Dugan, Claire Du Brey, Harry Tyler, Ralph Remley, and Zeffie Tilbury.
Directed by Irving Cummings, Produced by Darryl F. Zanuck, Screenplay by Lamar Trotti from a story by Ray Harris, Photographed by Leon Shamroy, Art Direction by Richard Day and Mark-Lee Karl, Music by Louis Silvers.
20th Century–Fox.

Tanganyika (1954) Color 81 minutes
Starring Van Heflin, Ruth Roman, Howard Duff, Jeff Morrow, Joe Comandore, Gregory Marshall, and Noreen Corcoran.
Directed by Andre de Toth, Produced by Albert J. Cohen, Screenplay by William Sackheim and Richard Alan Simmons, Photographed by Maury Gertsman, Art Direction by Eric Orbom, Music Direction by Joseph Gershenson.
Universal-International.

The Tattered Dress (1957) B&W/Scope 93 minutes
Starring Jeff Chandler, Jeanne Crain, Jack Carson, Gail Russell, Elaine Stewart, George Tobias, Edward Andrews, Philip Reed, and Edward C. Platt.
Directed by Jack Arnold, Produced by Albert Zugsmith, Screenplay by George Auckerman, Photographed by Carl E. Guthrie, Art Direction by Bill Newberry, Music by Frank Skinner.
Universal-International.

Terror in the Haunted House (1959) B&W/Psychorama 85 minutes
Starring Gerald Mohr, Cathy O'Donnell, William Ching, John Qualen, and Barry Bernard.
Directed by Harold Daniels, Produced by William S. Edwards, Screenplay by Robert C. Dennis, Photographed by Federick West, Art Direction by A. Leslie Thomas, Makeup by Harry Thomas, Music by Darrell Calker.
Howco International.

Terror Is a Man (1959) B&W 89 minutes
Starring Francis Lederer, Greta Thyssen, Richard Derr, Oscar Keesee, Lilia Duran, Peyton Keesee, and Flory Carlos.
Directed by Gerry De Leon, Produced by Kane Lynn and Eddie Romero, Screenplay by Harry Paul Harber from (uncredited) H.G. Wells' "Island of Dr. Moreau," Photographed by Emmanuel I. Rojas, Special Effects by Hilario Santos, Makeup by Remedios Amazon, Music by Ariston Auelino.
Valiant Films Corp.

That Night! (1957) B&W 88 minutes
Starring John Beal, Augusta Dabney, Shepperd Strudwick, Rosemary Murphy, Malcolm Broderick, Dennis Kohler, Beverly Lunsford, Bill Darrid, and Joe Julian.
Directed by John Newland, Produced by Himan Brown, Screenplay by Robert Wallace and Burton J. Rowles, Photographed by Maurice Hartzband, Art Direction by Melvin Bourne, Music by Mario Nascimbene.
RKO Radio Pictures/Universal-International Release.

13 Frightened Girls (1963) Color 89 minutes
Starring Kathy Dunn, Murray Hamilton, Joyce Taylor, Hugh Marlowe, Knigh Dhiegh, Lynne Sue Moon, Charlie Briggs, Norma Varden, Garth Benton, Maria Cristina Servera, Janet Mary Prance, Penny Anne Mills, Alexandra Lendon Bastedo, Ariane Glaser, Ilona Schutze, Anna Baj, Aiko Sakamoto, Judy Pace, Luz Gloria Hervias, Gina Trikonis, Marie-Louise Bielke, Ignacia Farias Luque, Emil Sitka, Jon Alvar, and Walter Rode.
Directed and Produced by William Castle, Screenplay by Robert Dillon from a story by Otis L. Guerney, Jr., Photographed by Gordon Avil, Art Direction by Don Ament, Makeup by Ben Lane, Music by Van Alexander.
Columbia.

13 Ghosts (1960) B&W/Partial Color/Illusion-O 88 minutes
Starring Charles Herbert, Donald Woods, Rosemary DeCamp, Martin Milner, Jo Morrow, Margaret Hamilton, and John Van Dreelan.
Directed and Produced by William Castle, Screenplay by Robb White, Photographed by Joseph Biroc, Art Direction by Cary Odell, Makeup by Ben Lane, Music by Von Dexter.
Columbia.

The 3 Worlds of Gulliver (1960) Color/SuperDynamation 100 minutes
Starring Kerwin Mathews, Jo Morrow, June Thorburn, Lee Patterson, Gregoire Aslan, Basil Sydney, Charles Lloyd Pack, Martin Benson, Mary Ellis, Marian Spencer, Peter Bull, Alex Mango, and Sherri Alberoni.
Directed by Jack Sher, Produced by Charles H. Schneer, Screenplay by Arthur Ross and Jack Sher based on "Gulliver's Travels" by Jonathan Swift,

Photographed by Wilkie Cooper, Art Direction by Gil Parrendo and Derek Barrington, Special Effects by Ray Harryhausen, Music by Bernard Herrmann. Columbia.

The Time Machine (1960) Color 103 minutes
Starring Rod Taylor, Alan Young, Yvette Mimieux, Sebastian Cabot, Tom Helmore, Whit Bissell, and Doris Lloyd.
Directed and Produced by George Pal, Screenplay by David Duncan based on the novel by H.G. Wells, Art Direction by George W. Davis and William Ferrari, Special Effects by Gene Warren, Wah Chang, Tim Baar, David Pal, Don Sahlin, Bill Brace, Makeup by Charles Cohram and Ron Berkeley, Music by Russell Garcia.
Metro-Goldwyn-Mayer.

The Tingler (1959) B&W (Partial Color) Percepto 80 minutes
Starring Vincent Price, Judith Evelyn, Darryl Hickman, Patricia Cutts, Philip Coolidge, Gail Bonney, Amy Fields, Clarence Straight, Pat Colby, Dal McKennon, and Bob Gunderson.
Directed and Produced by William Castle, Screenplay by Robb White, Photographed by Wilfrid M. Cline, Art Direction by Phil Bennett, Music by Von Dexter.
Columbia.

T-Men (1947) B&W 96 minutes
Starring Dennis O'Keefe, Mary Meade, Alfred Ryder, Wally Ford, June Lockhart, Charles McGraw, Jane Randolph, Art Smith, Herbert Heyes, Jack O'Verman, John Wengraf, Jim Bannon, and William Malter.
Directed by Anthony Mann, Produced by Aubrey Schenck, Screenplay by John C. Higgins from a story by Virginia Kellogg, Photographed by John Alton, Art Direction by Edward C. Jewell, Special Effects by George J. Teague and Jack Rabin, Music by Paul Sawtell.
Eagle Lion.

Torture Garden (1967) Color 93 minutes
Starring Jack Palance, Burgess Meredith, Beverly Adams, Peter Cushing, Robert Hutton, John Standing, Barbara Ewing, David Baur, Michael Ripper, Nicole Shelby, Bernard Kay, John Phillips, Catherine Finn, and Michael Hawkins.
Directed by Freddie Francis, Produced by Max J. Rosenberg and Milton Subotsky, Screenplay by Robert Bloch, Art Direction by Don Mingays and Scott Slimon, Makeup by Jill Carpenter, Music by Don Banks and James Bernard.

12 Angry Men (1957) B&W 95 minutes
Starring Henry Fonda, Lee J. Cobb, Ed Begley, E.G. Marshall, Jack Warden, Martin Balsam, John Fiedler, Jack Klugman, Edward Binns, Joseph

Sweeney, George Voskovec, Robert Webber, Rudy Bond, James A. Kelly, Bill Nelson, and John Savoca.

Directed by Sidney Lumet, Produced by Henry Fonda and Reginald Rose, Screenplay by Reginald Rose, Photographed by Robert Markell, Music by Kenyon Hopkins.

United Artists.

20,000 Leagues Under the Sea (1954) Color/Scope 127 minutes

Starring James Mason, Kirk Douglas, Paul Lukas, Peter Lorre, Robert Wilke, Carleton Young, Ted de Corsia, Percy Helton, and Red Cooper.

Directed by Richard Fleischer, Produced by Walt Disney, Screenplay by Earl Felton from the novel by Jules Verne, Art Direction by John Meehan and Harper Goff, Photographed by Franz Planer, Special Effects by John Hench and Ub Iwerks, Music by Paul Smith.

Buena Vista.

The Unholy Wife (1957) Color 94 minutes

Starring Diana Dors, Rod Steiger, Tom Tryon, Beulah Bondi, Marie Windsor, Tol Avery, Joe DeSantis, Gary Hunley, James Burke, and Louis Van Rooten.

Directed and Produced by John Farrow, Screenplay by Jonathan Latimer from a story by William Durkee, Photographed by Lucien Ballard, Art Direction by Franz Bachelin, Music by Daniele Amfitheatrof.

RKO Radio Pictures.

The Uninvited (1944) B&W 98 minutes

Starring Ray Milland, Ruth Hussey, Gail Russell, Donald Crisp, Cornelia Otis Skinner, Dorothy Stickney, Barbara Everest, Alan Napier, Ivan F. Simpson, Holmes Herbert, Jessie Newcomb, and Rita Page.

Directed by Lewis Allen, Produced by Charles Brackett, Screenplay by Dodie Smith and Frank Partos based on the novel by Dorothy Macardle, Photographed by Charles Lang, Art Direction by Ernst Fegte, Music by Victor Young.

Paramount.

Voice in the Mirror (1958) B&W/Scope 102 minutes

Starring Richard Egan, Julie London, Walter Matthau, Arthur O'Connell, Ann Doran, Bart Bradley, Hugh Sanders, Dorris Singleton, Casey Adams, Phil Harvey, and Mae Clarke.

Directed by Harry Keller, Produced by Gordon Kay, Screenplay by Larry Marcus, Photographed by William Daniels, Art Direction by Richard H. Riedel, Music by Henry Mancini.

Universal-International.

Wicked, Wicked (1973) Color/Duo-Vision 95 minutes
Starring David Bailey, Tiffany Bolling, Randolph Roberts, Scott Brady, Edd Byrnes, Diane McBain, Roger Bowen, Madeleine Sherwood, Indira Danks, Arthur O'Connell, Jack Knight, Patsy Garrett, Robert Nichols, Kirk Bates, Maryesther Denver.
Directed, Produced and Screenplay by Richard L. Bare, Photographed by Frederick Gately, Art Direction by Walter McKeegan, Makeup by Paul Stanhope, Music by Philip Springer.
Metro-Goldwyn-Mayer.

The Wild One (1953) B&W 79 minutes
Starring Marlon Brando, Mary Murphy, Robert Keith, Lee Marvin, Jay C. Flippen, Peggy Maley, Hugh Sanders, Ray Teal, John Brown, Will Wright, Robert Osterloh, Robert Bice, William Vedder, Yvonne Doughty, Keith Clarke, Gil Stratton, Jr., Darren Dublin, Johnny Tarangelo, Jerry Paris, Gene Peterson, Alvy Moore, Harry Landers, Jim Connell, Don Anderson, Angela Stevens, Bruno VeSoto, Pat O'Malley, and Tim Carey.
Directed by Laslo Benedek, Produced by Stanley Kramer, Screenplay by John Paxton from the story by Frank Rooney, Photographed by Hal Mohr, Art Direction by Walter Holscher, Music by Leith Stevens.
Columbia.

Witchcraft (1964) B&W 79 minutes
Starring Lon Chaney, Jack Hedley, Jill Dixon, Viola Keats, Marie Ney, David Weston, and Yvette Rees.
Directed by Don Sharp, Produced by Robert Lippert and Jack Parsons, Screenplay by Harry Spalding, Art Direction by George Provis.
20th Century–Fox.

Witness for the Prosecution (1957) B&W 114 minutes
Starring Tyrone Power, Marlene Dietrich, Charles Laughton, Elsa Lanchester, John Williams, Henry Daniell, Ian Wolfe, Una O'Connor, Torin Thatcher, Francis Compton, Norma Varden, Philip Tongue, and Ruta Lee.
Directed by Billy Wilder, Produced by Arthur Hornblow, Screenplay by Billy Wilder and Harry Kurnitz from the stage play by Agatha Christie, adapted by Larry Marcus, Photographed by Russell Harlan, Art Direction by Alexandre Trauner, Music by Matty Melneck.
United Artists.

The Wonderful World of the Brothers Grimm (1962) Color/Cinerama 129 minutes
Starring Laurence Harvey, Karl Boehm, Claire Bloom, Walter Slezak, Barbara Eden, Oscar Homolka, Arnold Stand, Martita Hunt, Ian Wolfe, Betty Garde, Cheerio Meredith, Bryan Russell, Tammy Marihugh, Walter Rilla,

Yvette Mimieux, Russ Tamblyn, Jim Backus, Beulah Bondi, Clinton Sundberg, Walter Brooke, Sandra Gale Bettin, Robert Foulk, Terry-Thomas, Buddy Hackett, Otto Kruger, Robert Crawford, Jr., Sydney Smith.

Directed by Henry Levin and George Pal, Produced by George Pal, Screenplay by David P. Harmon, Charles Beaumont and William Roberts based on "Die Bruder Grimm" by Dr. Hermann Gerstner, Photographed by C. Vogel, Art Direction by George W. Davis and Edward Carfagno, Special Effects by Gene Warren, Wah Chang, Tim Barr, Robert R. Hoag, and Jim Danforth, Music by Leigh Harline.

Metro-Goldwyn-Mayer.

"X" the Man with the X-Ray Eyes (1963) Color/Spectamation 80 minutes

Starring Ray Milland, Diana Van Der Vlis, Harold J. Stone, John Hoyt, Don Rickles, John Dierkes, Lorie Summers, Vicki Lee, Kathryn Hart, and Carol Irey.

Directed and Produced by Roger Corman, Screenplay by Robert Dillon and Ray Russell, Photographed by Floyd Crosby, Art Direction by Daniel Haller, Special Effects by Butler-Glouner, Inc., Makeup by Ted Coodley, Music by Les Baxter.

American International.

You Can't Take It with You (1938) B&W 127 minutes

Starring Jean Arthur, Lionel Barrymore, James Stewart, Edward Arnold, Mischa Auer, Ann Miller, Spring Byington, Samuel S. Hinds, Donald Meek, H.B. Warner, Halliwell Hobbes, Dub Taylor, Mary Forbes, Lilian Yarbo, Eddie Anderson, Clarence Wilson, Josef Swickard, Ann Doran, Christian Rub, Bodil Rosing, Charles Lane, and Harry Davenport.

Directed by Frank Capra, Screenplay by Robert Riskin based on the play by George S. Kaufman and Moss Hart, Photographed by Joseph Walker, Art Direction by Stephen Goosson, Music by Dimitri Tiomkin.

Columbia.

Zombies on Broadway (1945) B&W 68 minutes

Starring Wally Brown, Alan Carney, Bela Lugosi, Anne Jeffreys, Sheldon Leonard, Frank Jenks, Russell Hopton, Joseph Vitale, Ian Wolfe, Louis Jean Heydt, and Darby Jones.

Directed by Gordon Douglas, Produced by Ben Stoloff, Screenplay by Lawrence Kimble from a story by Robert Faver and Charles Newman, adapted by Robert E. Kent, Photographed by Jack Mackenzie, Art Direction by Albert S. D'Agostino and Walter E. Keller, Music by Roy Webb.

RKO Radio Pictures.

Zotz (1962) B&W 87 minutes

Starring Tom Poston, Julia Meade, Jim Backus, Fred Clark, Cecil Kellaway, Zeme North, Margaret Dumont, James Millhollin, Carl Don, Mike

Mazurki, Jimmy Hakins, Bart Patton, Judee Morton, Michael Westfield, Russ Whiteman, George Moorman, Elaine Martone, and Susan Dorn.

Directed and Produced by William Castle, Screenplay by Ray Russell from the novel by Walter Karig, Photographed by Gordon Avil, Art Direction by Robert Peterson, Makeup by Ben Lane, Music by Bernard Green.

Columbia.

Bibliography

Adair, Paul E. *Everthing You Wanted to Know About 3-D But Were Ashamed to Ask!* Texas, 1972.

Albert, Hollis. *The Dreams and the Dreamers.* New York, 1962.

Ardrey, Robert. "What Happened to Hollywood?" *The Reporter* (January 24, 1957), 17-18.

Bean, Robin, and David Austen. "USA: Confidential." *Films and Filming* (November, 1968), 16-31.

Bluestone, George. "In Defense of 3-D." *Seewanee Review* (Fall, 1956), 683-689.

Everitt, David. "Parasite." *The Bloody Best of Fangoria* (1983), 66-68.

Fiedler, Leslie. *An End to Innocence.* Boston, 1955.

Haver, Ronald. *David O. Selznick's Hollywood.* New York, 1980.

Hitchens, Gordon. "The Truth, The Whole Truth, and Nothing But the Truth About Exploitation Films." *Film Comment* (1964), 1-13.

Houseman, John. "Hollywood Faces the Fifties." *Harper's Magazine* (April, 1950), 50-59.

Keylin, Arleen, and Christine Bent. *The New York Times at the Movies.* New York, 1979.

Knight, Arthur. "Cheez It, the Cops!" *Saturday Review* (October, 1954), 43-44.

Knusch, Jim. "The History of Film Gimmicks, Part One." *Filmfax* (March/April, 1987), 10-12, 56-58.

————. "The History of Film Gimmicks, Part Two." *Filmfax* (June/July, 1987), 11-13, 52-55.

Laitin, Joseph. "Monsters Made to Order." *Colliers* (December, 1954), 52-53.

Legend, Johnny. "The World According to Wyott." *Fangoria* (October, 1984), 58-61, 64.

McCarthy, Todd, and Charles Flynn. *Kings of the Bs.* New York, 1975.

MacDonald, Dwight. "No Art and No Box Office." *Esquire* (March, 1959), 62-66.

MacGowan, Kenneth. *Behind the Screen.* New York, 1965.

Mandell, Paul. "Careers." *CineMagic* (Winter, 1987), 48-58.

Rebello, Stephen. "Selling Nightmares." *Cinefatastique* (March, 1988), 40-101.

Reilly, Rosa. "The Romance of the Vitaphone." *Screenland* (February, 1929), 46-47, 109-111.

"RKO: It's Only Money." *Fortune* (May, 1953), 122-127.

Shaffer, Helen B. "Movie-TV Competition." *Editorial Research Reports* (January 18, 1957), 43-61.

Stone, I.F. *The Haunted Fifties.* New York, 1963.

Swires, Steve. "Farewell to Fantasy Films." *Starlog* (February, 1988), 63-67.

Thomas, Bob. *King Cohn.* New York, 1967.

Thornshaw, Brick. "Joe Alves and Jaws 3D." *Fangoria* (September, 1983), 44-47.

Warner, Jack. *My First Hundred Years in Hollywood.* New York, 1965.

Warshow, Robert. *The Immediate Experience.* New York, 1962.

Weales, Gerald. "Crazy, Mixed-up Kids Take Over." *The Reporter,* (December 13, 1956), 40-41.

Weldon, Michael. *The Psychotronic Encyclopedia of Film.* New York, 1983.

Williams, Sharon, and Al Taylor. "The Creature Talks Among Us!" *Filmfax* (October/November, 1986), 41-46.

Index

Boldface numbers indicate photos or illustrations.

N

O